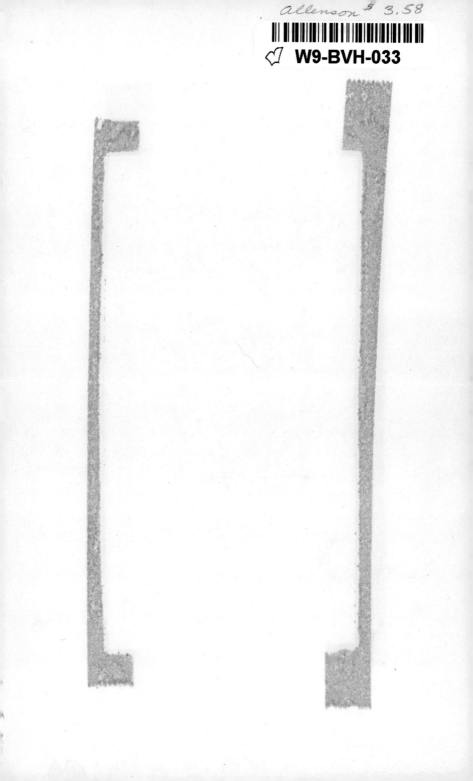

Pastor Martin Niemöller, a portrait by Knud Knudsen

Martin Niemöller

PASTOR NIEMÖLLER

DIETMAR SCHMIDT

Translated from the German by
LAWRENCE WILSON

DOUBLEDAY & COMPANY, INC.
Garden City, New York
1959

Library of Congress Catalog Card Number 59-12275
Copyright © 1959 by Dietmar Schmidt
All Rights Reserved
Printed in the United States of America

CONTENTS

PREFACE   *page* 9

Chapter 1. EARLY YEARS (1892–1910)   13

2. U-BOAT COMMANDER (1910–18)   27

3. MARRIAGE AND THE MINISTRY
   (1918–23)   57

4. THE WESTPHALIAN HOME MISSION
   (1923–31)   73

5. PASTOR *versus* STATE (1931–6)   83

6. TRIAL FOR TREASON (1936–45)   101

7. COLLAPSE OF GERMANY (1945)   130

8. IN SEARCH OF WORLD PEACE
   (1945–7)   140

9. PERSONAL PORTRAIT   194

BIOGRAPHICAL NOTES   214

BIBLIOGRAPHY   218

ILLUSTRATIONS

Pastor Martin Niemöller, a portrait by
    Knud Knudsen   *Frontispiece*

With Hermann Bremer when a cadet in the
    Imperial Navy   *facing*   28

With his fiancée Else Bremer at Elberfeld   58

St. Anne's Church, Dahlem   82

At the Consecration of Pastor von Bodelschwingh
    as Reich Bishop, 1933   86

Pastor Niemöller at Dahlem   98

With his son Martin ("Tini")   102

Hitler's personal prisoner   134

Preaching in Basle   150

"Procession of Witness," Sydney, 1949   156

Hertha Niemöller   182

With Mr. Nehru and Dr. Visser't Hooft, 1953   186

Pastor and Mrs. Niemöller in Honolulu, 1949   194

Jochen Niemöller   206

Dora and Ratz   210

Receiving an honorary degree from
    Dr. Rajendra Prasad   212

PREFACE

IT is no easy task to write about a man when his life's journey is not yet ended and no one can tell where it will lead him. The task becomes even harder when that man is Niemöller, for the mere mention of the name in both East and West Germany today is enough to start an argument based on every feeling and prejudice ranging from fervid admiration to implacable repudiation.

The matter is not simplified by the fact that, on close examination, the man Niemöller is seen not to fit into any of the pigeonholes to which he has been assigned, either for the sake of convenience or because people fail to understand him. In the words of his scarcely less controversial friend, the Swiss theologian Karl Barth: "To the orthodox he is too worldly, to the liberals, too clerical, to the socialists, too militaristic, and all of us find him too much of a Prussian."

What is the essential Niemöller? What is he trying to achieve? Is he the "black sheep in the political life of post-war Germany," or a "German Gandhi"? Is he a "disturbing and disruptive element," or "the modern Jeremiah" and "the symbol of a militant Protestantism"? Niemöller himself does not always make it easy for his contemporaries and even for his friends to understand him. "What we admire about him is that he is continually destroying his own fame", one of his French friends has said, and thereby come very close perhaps to the crux of the "Niemöller problem."

This "destruction" of his own fame does in fact seem characteristic of Niemöller. Though the life he leads is outwardly as varied, dramatic and exciting as any novel, he is nevertheless no suitable object for uncritical hero-worship, and to judge by the shocks, paradoxes and seeming illogicalities which he so frequently flings at the public, he would seem not to want to be.

Any attempt to set Niemöller up as a hero is bound to lead us far from the spot where the key to his life lies buried. And the reading of reports with sensational sentences lifted individually from his speeches can only distort the picture of this life. The thread which runs through Niemöller's life with increasing clarity, and which so few of his critics or admirers discern, must be sought elsewhere. Anyone who takes the trouble to read or listen to one of his sermons will have no difficulty in finding it, for he will discover that the former U-boat commander, whose aggressive temperament and disdain of tactics or diplomacy is a frequent source of annoyance to those with whom he comes in contact, aims only to be a mouthpiece of a cause whose protagonists, he believes, have to come to terms with the "world," but in doing so must make no sacrifice of principle. "The Evangel is attack" stood on one of his postcards from Hitler's concentration camp. Here lies the "thread" in Niemöller's life, and the clarification of many misunderstandings could start from this point.

The author knows that this first sizable biography of Martin Niemöller is incomplete and provisional, but he hopes it may contribute, though only modestly, to the removal of these misunderstandings. It is addressed in the first place to the non-theologians among Niemöller's critics, friends and critical friends. The author has refrained as far as possible from embarking on the questionable process of "interpretation," that eternal temptation and pitfall of the professional historian whom, in any case, he has no desire to emulate. For more perhaps than any other human undertaking, is not the attempt to portray a period of history or an individual human life "as it really was," perpetually doomed to remain no more than—an attempt?

DIETMAR SCHMIDT

Oberursel Taunus,
  April, 1958

10

PASTOR NIEMÖLLER

Chapter One

EARLY YEARS

(1892–1910)

MARTIN NIEMÖLLER is a Westphalian, and Westphalians can be awkward people. Noted for their self-reliance and dependability, they refuse to be rushed and cannot be browbeaten. Some call them stubborn; others, obstinate, but all are agreed that once he has made up his mind the Westphalian is slow to change it. It took Charlemagne forty years to subdue his ancestors, the Low Saxons, and compel them to become Christians. Jerome, Bonaparte's brother, found them refractory and disrespectful subjects. The Romans had long since discovered the same—and something more: "*Westphalus est sine pietate, sine pudore, conscientia, veritate* . . ."

"Impious, shameless—but conscientious and truthful . . ." Thus the Westphalian appeared to the foreign overlord. Amongst his own people some of these characteristics would have different names and he would be respected as a man full of filial piety and faithful to religious tradition, resolute in defence of his pagan gods and not ashamed to be thought a barbarian. "He's a Westphalian . . ." Even today the phrase is often heard in Germany and it calls to mind a picture, varying in minor details, but definite enough to prompt the rejoinder: "Ah! That explains it . . .," either spoken or implied by pursed lips and a knowing air. The speakers look at the back—a broad back—of their friend and think of that heavy, sometimes rather dour expression on his face. He takes life seriously, is shrewd and heavy going until he has had a drink or two inside him. Then he shuts up like

13

an oyster. He is not the man to let fall an unguarded word. But when he makes up his mind to speak, then people listen. He can be terrifyingly blunt. And the two men think of the story, apocryphal perhaps, but none the less illustrative of the Westphalian character.

It was in the days of Jerome, "King" of Westphalia, if you please! King Frolic, they called him, because all he thought about was having a good time, while his brother's victories kept him on his throne. Naturally, the Westphalians hated him and he would not have lasted for twenty-four hours if it had not been or that pale-faced little demon, his brother, and the fact that they were too poor to risk having their farms burnt down all over again by the French. Besides, the Westphalians were not like other men; some of them were gifted with the second sight and had seen, when the mood was on them, a great battlefield with the Imperial Guard lying, men and horses, in a sea of blood and the little Corsican, his face as pale as wax, weeping as the sun went down. They could not tell when it would be, that ultimate defeat, but they knew it would come and they could wait. But meanwhile, Napoleon was winning victories everywhere. The latest one had been followed by an order from King Jerome that thanksgiving services were to be held in every church throughout Westphalia; the pastors were to preach a sermon thanking God for the "victory" and a Te Deum was to be sung. To Pastor Schliepstein of the Great Church of St. Mary in Lippstadt this order brought the last and final blow to his self-restraint and he made up his mind it was time to speak. He chose the text for his "thanksgiving" sermon from Isaiah: "Because thy rage against me and thy tumult is come up into mine ears, therefore will I put my hook in thy nose and my bridle on thy lips and I will turn thee back by the way by which thou camest." His brief but pungent sermon kept closely to this text and after expressly stating its relevance to the situation then prevailing, closed with the words: "And before long I hope we shall be singing the Te Deum for very different reasons." The service

14

concluded, Pastor Schliepstein found the French commissioner waiting for him in his vestry. He wanted a copy of the sermon. But, strangely enough, the pastor had made no notes. "In these times we find it unnecessary," he said blandly. . . . Long afterwards, Martin Niemöller's father was to become pastor of that same parish.

Living in the north-west plains of Germany close to the Dutch frontier amidst a flat and somewhat mournful countryside, the people of Westphalia have been peasants and small farmers since the earliest times. Martin Niemöller's great-grandfather had been a farmer in the small village of Wersen, not far from Osnabrück. His forebears also had lived by the soil, some of them—as the name Niemöller implies—being millers.

Martin's grandfather, on the other hand, had shown an early talent for book learning and had been sent to a teachers' training college. For twenty-five years until his death, he had been schoolmaster and organist in the parish of Wersen—the two posts usually went together—and in addition, sexton and latterly, churchwarden. The village sexton was something of a personage in those days. He was entitled to free accommodation at the expense of the parish and to a parcel of land comprising meadow and coppice. Nevertheless, Gerhard Niemöller's annual salary—the equivalent of £38, of which twenty shillings was for "touching the organ" twice weekly in church—was barely enough to feed and clothe his eight children, and their principal diet consisted of rye bread and potatoes, while none of them ever had a winter overcoat. The family possessions were correspondingly meagre and did not include even an alarm clock, with the result that when the father had to get up particularly early, for example on Christmas Day to ring the church bell for early service, two of his children had to take it in turns to stay awake all night so that one of them could rouse him at the first light of dawn.

Martin Niemöller's grandfather was never robust and he died at the age of fifty-four, almost twenty years before his grandson was born. His wife Christine, on the other hand, had an iron constitution. Born and bred in a village not far from Wersen, she spent most of her long life within an area of a few square miles ánd she was seventy before she took her first railway journey. As a girl in her parents' home she had never known the luxury of an oil lamp by which to read in the evenings: the fire was the only source of illumination and by its flickering light she had studied in winter and learned by heart some scores of hymns which later she taught to her grandchildren. Yet to the day she died at the age of eighty-one she never needed spectacles and throughout most of her life she was accustomed to get up at dawn. Martin's grandmother was also a woman of dauntless fortitude. On her husband's death the privileges he had enjoyed as sexton, including free accommodation, passed to his successor and his widow was faced with the necessity of providing her children with a roof over their heads, apart from contriving somehow to earn enough to support them. This double problem Christine solved at a blow by building herself a small house on the outskirts of Wersen and then starting a grocer's shop in one of the rooms. It was thanks to their mother's unaided efforts that the children, including Martin's father, were launched on their careers and to Christine's devotion as a mother, no less than to their inherited strength of physique, that seven of the eight brothers and sisters lived to be over seventy.

Heinrich Niemöller, Martin's father, was an Evangelical pastor. Born in 1859, he entered the Church at the age of twenty-seven, married when he was thirty and died in 1941, during the Second World War, at the age of eighty-two. While still a boy he was known to his family as "the little pastor", and he himself apparently never doubted that he was destined for the Ministry, —and destined in the most literal sense, for throughout his life he remained convinced that Almighty God took a personal interest in his affairs, intervening decisively at moments of crisis to supply yet further proof, if such were needed, of His eternal benevolence. Today such an attitude may be regarded as naïve, even arrogant, yet to Heinrich Niemöller, as to countless of his contemporaries, the belief in God as ever present and ever concerned for the welfare of each individual human being was a constant source of inspiration and strength. Such men could pray: "Our Father . . ."—and mean it.

In the case of Heinrich Niemöller, his religious faith seems to have been innate rather than acquired. Almost as soon as he could read, the Bible stories kindled his childish imagination and made him long to visit the Holy Land, a wish which was later to be fulfilled. A man of simple tastes but generous enthusiasms, holding a limited number of robust, straightforward opinions, methodical, conscientious to a degree, forthright, unsubtle though never complacent, he made an excellent pastor, tireless in both practising and preaching the fundamentals of the Evangelical creed: faith and good works.

During the forty-five years of his ministry he preached many thousands of sermons in no less than five hundred towns and villages, and to the end of his days, whether in his own church or as a guest preacher in some other parish, he continued to draw packed congregations. And yet, as he once confessed in old age: "I have never mounted a pulpit without a pounding heart." If this nervousness had contained any thought for himself, he would have got over it, but it was based on humility, not on conceit, and on a full sense of the importance and responsibility of preaching God's Word. It was because he was so patently sincere that Heinrich Niemöller was so successful as a preacher. He had something very definite to say and he took pains to ensure that his congregations heard and understood it. Natural in delivery, clear and incisive in manner, he never preached extempore. Every one of his sermons was written out in full and at the end of each year his manuscripts were bound and placed on the bookshelf beside the sermons of previous years. At the time of his death they filled more than fifty volumes. Heinrich Niemöller once tried to enshrine the secret of his success as a preacher in six words. A good sermon, he maintained, should be "audible, agreeable and appetizing: direct, deliberate and dignified."

To us living in an age of doubt, Heinrich Niemöller appears as a man of positively monolithic compactness and simplicity, consistent in his beliefs and actions to a degree which, even if we would, most of us could never emulate. His lifelong loyalty to the House of Hohenzollern will serve as an example. The first time he saw the Emperor William II was in 1892, when the Emperor attended the re-dedication of Martin Luther's church in Wittenberg. Surrounded by a posse of princelings, heralded by fanfares and attended by a guard of honour, in the eyes of the Westphalian pastor, no doubt, the Emperor personified all the might and magnificence of the young German Empire, at that time scarcely more than twenty years old. In an ecstasy of patriotism, the pastor flung his cap high into the air—to watch it sail over the heads of the crowd and land in the midst of the Imperial Guard of Honour. To the end of his days Heinrich Niemöller enjoyed quoting the comment of the captain in charge. "*Herr Pfarrer!*" called the officer. "Enthusiasm is all very well, but you've ruined my dressing!" To which Niemöller would add: "But I would do the same again. . . !"

One more memory of Kaiser William, this time in Jerusalem in 1898. Heinrich Niemöller's dream had come true and he was on a visit to the Holy Land when the Emperor arrived, fresh from a State visit to the Sultan Abdul Hamid of Turkey, to attend the consecration of a new German Evangelical church. Once more, as Niemöller watched the resplendent figure, he was swept with intense, quasi-mystical emotion and whole sentences from the Emperor's speech became engraved on his mind. "If we hold fast to the teaching of the Gospels," the Kaiser declared, "not even the gates of Hell shall prevail against our beloved Evangelical Church." And later, in the same speech: "It is neither glory, nor power, nor fame, nor honour that we seek here—nor any earthly prize, for our heart is set on a greater— the salvation of our souls. That is the object of all our striving, of our most ardent desire and of our prayerful supplications." Long after the Emperor was dead, between air raids during the Second World War, Heinrich Niemöller recalled these words with approval, seeing again as he did so the glittering helmets and the brilliant uniforms of Imperial Germany, and the Emperor himself, the august symbol of her power. And who could blame him for looking back with nostalgia in 1941 to those years before Armageddon, when the disasters of the twentieth century were yet to come, and the newly united Germany was beginning to show the world her people's unique capacity for disciplined hard work?

In 1889, the year of Heinrich Niemöller's marriage, after he had taken up his first appointment as pastor of a parish, Germany was entering a period of unprecedented economic expansion. From being a minor participant in international trade, in the space of fifteen years she was to become Britain's foremost competitor, outstripping even the United States in the speed of her industrialization. Exports were doubled and redoubled, the national income increased, and with home prices lagging behind the upward trend of wages, the standard of living improved. Health improved. Slum clearance was started, and slowly legislation was set in hand to provide social security for the growing army of industrial workers.

Moreover, in 1889 Kaiser William II had only just ascended the throne. As yet Bismarck was still at the helm, skilfully fostering the rivalries between Germany's neighbours so that the balance of power could be maintained and the youthful empire grow to manhood unmolested. Even after the Chancellor's resignation in the following year, it was some time before the Emperor's instability of character, his reckless moods and constant shifts of policy at last caused Germany's western neighbours to concert together and, with the equilibrium so carefully sustained by Bismarck destroyed, the first faint signs of the gathering storm appeared above the distant horizon. For a few more years, prosperity increased and progress continued under cloudless skies. It was in this period that Martin Niemöller was born.

Martin's father had first met his future wife when she was still a child. Her name was Paula Müller and her father ran a general store in the small town of Westerkappeln, not far from Wersen. When they married, Heinrich Niemöller had recently been appointed pastor of Lippstadt at the early age of thirty. His bride was twenty-one.

The young, vivacious girl differed in many respects from the more integrated teacher's and sexton's son from the village of Wersen. While Heinrich Niemöller, despite his sense of humour, gave a quiet, staid, almost partriarchal impression, his wife was emotional and artistically inclined. Though she herself was a Westphalian, her ancestors had been strangers to Westphalia: she had French blood in her veins. Her mother's maiden name had been Graes and her forebears had emigrated from their Belgian or, possibly, French home to Westphalia on account of their Protestant faith. They had settled at first in the city of Münster, but had then moved farther west.

Thereafter the family suffered considerable hardship and, lacking the means to keep up their position, they renounced their title of nobility and changed the name from De Graes to Graes. But they remained proud of their Huguenot ancestry and continued to cherish its traditions. Many years later, it gave Paula Niemöller's son, Martin, great satisfaction when, as a grown and already famous man, he found mention of her family name when travelling in southern France. It appeared on a memorial tablet erected in memory of Protestants who had been sentenced to the galleys in the time of the Counter-Reformation. It is possible, therefore, that, like their twentieth-century descendant, Martin Niemöller's ancestors were made to suffer cruel hardship for their Protestant faith.

This Huguenot tradition of which Paula Niemöller's family were so proud included highly developed intellectual and artistic interests, particularly in the sphere of literature. Researches conducted by Paula Niemöller's step-sister, Alwine, revealed that one of their ancestors living in the neighbourhood of Holtwick in Westphalia in the fifteenth century had achieved some fame as a Professor of Philosophy, while Alwine herself could remember having seen their grandfather reading French books with much interest. He had been bilingual in French and German, a fact which would have helped the local schoolmistress to understand the remarkably idiomatic and accurate French which his granddaughters managed to produce in their homework! Alwine also recalled a mysterious coffer belonging to her grandfather which was decorated with the De Graes coat-of-arms. The old man must have been an impressive figure with his fine forehead, aquiline nose and penetrating blue eyes. He was over eighty when he grumblingly accepted a seat on the town council, but once installed, he made his presence felt, arguing with a voluble charm aided, when the tactics of debate so required, by an assumed air of senile intractability. Alwine had vivid memories of the old man returning from these meetings of the town council pink-cheeked and bright-eyed after some furious tussle with his colleagues. But they respected him, all the same.

The newly-fledged pastor's wife, Paula Niemöller, brought all her grandfather's energy to her new tasks and in the course of the years she developed a rare talent as an assistant to Heinrich in his public duties as well as in the home. She was one of those beings who seem to thrive on incessant activity. The more energy she expended, the greater her reserves seemed to grow. Making garments for the poor of the parish, decorating the church for the Christmas and Easter celebrations, painting hundreds of Easter eggs in bright colours for distribution in the parish, and above all, bearing, feeding, controlling, admonishing and encouraging her ever growing family. . . . Paula Niemöller was indeed one of the mainstays of life for countless people, and some might have taken advantage of her inexhaustible goodwill if her husband had not made it clear at an early stage that her main duties were in the home. In a welcoming speech to the new pastor and his bride, a representative of the parish turned to her and indicated the wealth of rewarding work which awaited her. In his reply, Pastor Niemöller gave suitable expression to his gratitude for the opportunities extended, and then, with a glance at his wife, added: "But, gentlemen, happy as she will be to do all and more than is asked of her, I would have you remember that she is my wife —not yours!"

Both Heinrich Niemöller and his wife came from large families and their memories of their own childhood and the methods employed by their parents in bringing up their children no doubt helped them to avoid an exaggerated application of theory when it came to rearing a family of their own. They seem to have avoided most of the familiar pitfalls: an over-anxious solicitude on the one hand, aloofness on the other. They implanted in them none of those complexes which are so often the product of a "Christian" upbringing. They ensured that their children did not form an exclusive attachment to either parent —or, rather, the danger never existed because both Heinrich and Paula loved their children and yet at the same time respected their right to be separate and distinct individuals, so that the expression of their love was not possessive or stifling, but acceptable to their family who, like all children, required protection without domination and at the same time freedom to become strong and independent individuals.

For sixteen years the Niemöllers lived in Lippstadt—*die liebe Stadt* as Heinrich called it—and there, in the ancient, rambling vicarage with its massive beams, gigantic chimneys and creaking floor-boards, five of their six children were born: the first, Heinrich, in 1890, who died in 1894; then Martin, in 1892; then Magdalene, Pauline and Wilhelm.

The first eight years of Martin's life were spent in idyllic surroundings. As soon as he could walk there was the big garden at the back of the vicarage to explore with Tell, the family sheep-dog—lawns, fruit-trees, flower beds, and doves cooing among the branches on hot summer days. Later, the horses belonging to neighbouring farmers became an attraction, and a river that ran right across the bottom of the garden, the River Lippe from which the town took its name, swirling, gliding, eddying past with all the mystery and enchantment that lie in moving waters. Here the parson's son and his friends played and watched as the river ran with the seasons, clear and sparkling under open skies in summertime, leaden in winter, and it was here, as he followed the stream in imagination until it joined the Rhine and the Rhine moved, slowly widening, westwards towards Holland, that Martin first heard the call of the sea.

But with Heinrich Niemöller often absent from home on Church business or preaching in some other parish, his wife saw to it that the children were properly disciplined. "We were free —on a long leash," Martin Niemöller recalls. Reinforcing parental restraint, the regular routine of the vicarage and the church services, and not least, Heinrich Niemöller's tidy mind and orderly habits set the children an example in self-discipline and showed them that if life is to be lived, it must be organized.

In those days a pastor of a parish and his family enjoyed considerable prestige in the community. This was particularly the case in Lippstadt where the part played by the town in the Reformation was still a matter for local pride. In the sixteenth century Johann Westermann, a monk in the monastery of St. Augustine, had journeyed to Wittenberg to meet Martin Luther and study his teaching at first hand. He returned home a convinced adherent and quickly succeeded in converting the inhabitants of Lippstadt and neighbourhood to the Protestant cause, thereby gaining the title, "The Reformer of Lippstadt". It is said that Luther himself visited the town in 1522 and preached in one of the three churches. Whether or not that is true, it is an undoubted fact that Lippstadt was the first town in Westphalia to accept the New Teaching. Since then the majority of the inhabitants have been Protestants, jealously guarding the traditions of their faith. Martin Niemöller thus grew up in an atmosphere of something more than conventional Protestantism.

Martin was eight and had been attending primary school in Lippstadt for over two years when he was abruptly torn from the scenes of his childhood. In the year 1900 his father received an unexpected invitation to become pastor of Elberfeld, a town in the heart of the industrial area of Rhineland-Westphalia. Some years previously, while travelling through with his wife, he had remarked: "Thank God I'm not pastor here!" Now, for some reason, he felt inclined to accept, but first, there was a small difficulty to surmount. It was made a condition of his appointment that he should preach a trial sermon in Elberfeld. Heinrich Niemöller's reply is on record. It was as blunt as a Westphalian could make it. "If I don't know how to preach a sermon by now, I shall certainly never learn to do so with you." On receipt of this refusal, the Elberfelders unanimously waived the condition and on 15 November, 1900, Heinrich Niemöller and his family said good-bye to Lippstadt.

The contrast between peaceful Lippstadt and the teeming industrial town could hardly have been greater and Martin, for one, was not edified. The vicarage turned out to be a gloomy modern red-brick building. There was no garden and though the turbid stream that struggled through the valley was called a river and it, too, was a tributary of the Rhine, it summoned no visions of the sea, but only such pictures appropriate to Wuppertal, the "Valley of the Wuppe". Martin's disgust was unbounded and he summed it all up in one sentence: "Father, weren't you *stupid* to leave Lippstadt!"

Heinrich Niemöller's new parish of 6000 souls was at the very heart of Germany's great industrial expansion and within a decade, Elberfeld itself, together with the neighbouring town of Barmen, lost its identity and became a suburb of Wuppertal, swelling the latter's population to near the half-million mark. Meanwhile, the new pastor had plenty to do. While the newspapers talked of the Boxer Rebellion, the new Chancellor, Count von Bülow, and the occupation by German troops of the Chinese port of Kiao-Chow, Heinrich Niemöller systematically set about getting to know his parishioners, visiting them in their homes at the rate of 1800 a year. Martin, too, was kept busy and soon he was settling down at the Elberfeld Grammar School and acquiring an interest in subjects which were new to him—Greek, French, mathematics and physics. Out of school, he was developing a passion for gymnastics, in those days the principal form of organized exercise, and before long his school-fellows had elected him to the coveted position of "Vorturner", or demonstrator and leader in their gymnastic displays. As time passed the memories of Lippstadt—*die liebe Stadt*—began to lose their painful associations of an idyllic life that had gone, never to return.

While his brother and sisters, now increased by a baby girl, worked and had their being on the second floor of the barrack-like vicarage in the Arrenbergerstrasse, Martin sat in his private domain under the roof. One of the attic windows looked out on to the steeple of the Church of the Holy Trinity and through the other he could see clear sky. Here he did his homework, or sat gazing at the strange wallpaper he had contrived out of pictures of ships cut from newspapers and magazines and stuck at random over every square inch of plaster. Sometimes when the rain was drumming on the roof of the dormer windows and the wind began to moan round his eyrie, he would imagine himself at sea on the bridge of a warship, a member of his Imperial Majesty's Navy.

Martin first set eyes on the sea in 1908, when he was sixteen. His father had arranged for him to spend six weeks in England as the guest of a Dr. Lumb and his family in London. His hosts turned out to be exceedingly devout. They went to church twice on Sundays and refused to allow Martin to play the piano on the Sabbath. Even Beethoven was banned, as being "too worldly a composer". Martin was amazed, but polite enough to conceal his surprise. In the evenings, Dr. Lumb and his family would ply him with questions about Germany, thus helping him to improve his English, or they would read Shakespeare, seated round the fire in picturesque and carefully adjusted attitudes so that they could all overlook the text. The son of the house taught Martin to play billiards; and one morning, between Hyde Park Corner and Piccadilly Circus, he fell in love with a girl sitting opposite him in the bus. He travelled the same route at the same time for days after, but he never saw her again—the girl with the fair, curly hair and the china-blue eyes—and as he became immersed in sightseeing, he found he could not remember whether her eyes had been blue or hazel.

During those six weeks Martin explored London with unabating curiosity. Each morning after breakfast he took a horse-drawn bus from the suburb where he was staying to visit St. Paul's, the Tower of London, the Houses of Parliament, Westminster Abbey, or some other famous building. He solemnly toured the National Gallery, and then the Tate Gallery. He drove out to inspect Windsor and Hampton Court and took a tram to the White City to see the recently opened Anglo-French Exhibition, wandering dazedly amongst a sea of flowers and bunting, past monster statues in plaster of Paris and Venetian scenes with real water and plywood façades. When he was tired of art or architecture he would repair to a teashop and restore his energies with steak-and-kidney pudding followed by strawberry flan with vanilla sauce. Sometimes after he had found the phrase in his dictionary, he would ask for "a second helping" of the flan, for his father had given him three pounds pocket money and he had never felt so wealthy before. Then, reinvigorated, Martin would somehow always feel the urge to take one more look at the river and he would go down to the Thames and wangle his way on to one of the jetties by Tower Bridge. There, as he watched the ships glide downstream in the autumn evening and the lights came up gleaming gold through the mist, he would sniff the air and convince himself that even at that distance he could smell the sea.

Chapter Two

U-BOAT COMMANDER

(1910–18)

IN March, 1910, Martin Niemöller became a cadet in the Imperial German Navy. The transition from school playground to barrack square was abrupt. Martin had barely got over the end-of-term supper with its beer and buffoonery when the order to report for naval training dropped into the family letter-box. Then his boyhood dreams of a life on the ocean wave faded before the harsh realities of the Flensburg-Mürwik Naval Training College. The principle in those days was to give the young gentlemen a shock at the very start of their training, thereby sorting out the sheep from the goats. Those that stayed the course might one day turn out to be useful sailors—the rest could go home. Meanwhile, as temporary cadets only, they drilled and marched and about-turned, sweating with exertion and blushing with shame as they were picked out, one by one, for the fruity sarcasms of their instructor.

After six weeks, the temporary gentlemen were considered fit to be seen by the Commanding Officer, Vice-Admiral Coerper, and on 7 May, the dreaded General Inspection was held. After taking the oath in the Garrison Church in Kiel, the victims proudly emerged from their ordeal as fully fledged cadets entitled henceforth to the nickname of *Pünktchen*, or "Pimples". Those that disliked the name claimed that it had something to do with the cockade in their caps which was unadorned with oak-leaves. The remainder humbled themselves to accept a more obvious derivation.

There followed a short Whitsun leave and then the Pimples joined the training ship, *Hertha*, at Kiel. Afloat at last, their spirits revived. At least, they told themselves, there would be no more presenting arms. If they suffered, it would be in a good cause. The *Hertha* was one of four armoured cruisers used at that time for training purposes. The course lasted a year. A bare three weeks of theoretical instruction, P.T. and boat-pulling, and the *Hertha* sailed for her North Sea and Mediterranean training cruise taking fifty fortunate Pimples with her. These cruises were considered an essential part of a naval officer's training. They broadened his mind as well as teaching him the difficult art of living amicably and efficiently in the narrow confines of a ship.

On 2 June, 1910, the *Hertha* sailed past the lightship at Brunsbüttel and headed for the open sea. On the very first day, the Pimples had a breath-taking experience when they sailed past the German High Seas Fleet, headed by the battleship *Deutschland*. Their first foreign port of call was Skagen in Denmark. The Danish torpedo-boat, *Makrelen*, with whom they exchanged salutes, called forth the critical attention of the young seamen. In his log Cadet Niemöller classed her perfunctorily as "no good" —"because she does only 19·5 knots ". A red question-mark in the margin showed that his superior officer noted he had yet to learn the difference between wisdom and prejudice.

Cadet Niemöller's log-book, a stout tome, its originally white label now yellow with age, still survives to remind its owner of those halcyon days. Within are ready ruled pages with spaces in which to note such details as course and speed of the ship, position in longitude and latitude, time, weather conditions, wind speed, barometer readings and air temperature. Then follows the day-to-day recordings of events, from 2 June, 1910 to 13 April, 1911. Part Two is headed by a list of cadets under training, dockyard apprentices also under training, and the names of "the staff of H.I.M. cruiser *Hertha*".

The cruise in northern waters lasted ten weeks, until mid-

Martin Niemöller with his friend, and later brother-in-law, Hermann Bremer, when they were cadets together in the Imperial German Navy

August, 1910, the places visited including Denmark, Sweden and the Norwegian fiords. After a brief and strenuous interval in Kiel spent in coaling and taking on stores, the cruise was resumed southwards, calling at Plymouth, San Sebastian, Tangier, Barcelona, Tunis, Port Said, Alexandria, Haifa, and on the return journey, Venice, Corfu and Genoa. For the Pimples life on board was hard but seldom monotonous. There was no time for tedium. Apart from P.T. and fencing lessons to keep them fit—as though they needed it!—they were put through an endless round of instruction: gunnery, navigation, communication drill, signalling by morse and semaphore, watch-keeping and elementary engineering. On top of all this, they rehearsed the drill for "man overboard" until they could do it in their sleep, and just as well, for often enough the alarm would be sounded in the middle of the night and they would have to scramble straight from their hammocks into the boats. But what did it matter? They were young and, in that summer of 1910, all was new to them. Even kit inspection aroused their competitive spirit. This was their career.

Shore leave or a break in the routine were the signals for wild rejoicing. There were many such occasions, all carefuly noted in his log by Cadet Niemöller. Soon after the start of the cruise, for example, they met the German pleasure steamer, *Meteor*. Boats were lowered and the trippers were allowed to swarm over the ship. In Barcelona a party was given on board for members of the German Club. Off Majorca the cadets exchanged visits with the British sailors from H.M.S. *Cumberland*. "A grand evening" records the log, "very enjoyable", "most friendly". Off Port Said, the German Crown Prince and Princess came on board from the liner in which they were sailing to India. In Alexandria, the *Hertha* was beseiged by dark-skinned, disreputable looking natives selling carpets, fruit, cigarettes. On shore leave in the Austrian port of Cattaro, two cadets unwittingly crossed the frontier into Montenegro and were punished with two days' "light arrest".

When the ship called at Corfu, the officers went hunting in Albania and returned with some snipe and a wild boar. In Pola they met the entire Austrian Fleet—more parties, or, as the log-book has it, "a very bright and friendly afternoon".

No event on board the *Hertha* was too insignificant to be included in the log. "Lieutenant Schaarschmidt promoted Lieut. Commander", we read under 20 November, 1910; and elsewhere, "Boatswain's Mate Ertz today promoted to Boatswain's Mate 1st Class." Nor were less agreeable experiences passed over. In Plymouth, Niemöller experienced his first punishment. As coxswain of the picket-boat maintaining contact between ship and shore, he cast off so clumsily that the line fouled the picket-boat's propeller. By way of penalty, his watch was extended to midnight; the following day he had to report to his superior officer, who gave him an hour's punishment drill. But that afternoon, none the worse, he was with a party of liberty men sailing up the River Tamar in the paddle-steamer *Britannia*.

The Pimples' pet aversion was coaling. They hated every minute of it, the more so in that it was a torture specially devised as part of their training programme. Sack by grimy sackful they solemnly transferred a heap of coal from the quayside to the bunkers of the ship. That done, they embarked on an orgy of washing, so regaining, as the log tells us, "a more or less human appearance".

Then one day, in the neighbourhood of Bergen, young Niemöller's heart gave a lurch as he read the name on a passing British steamer: *Midnight Sun*. The cadets gazed at her indifferently—they had seen better, they had seen worse, and she needed a coat of paint. But that night Niemöller wrote in his log: "In this ship my father took part in the Emperor's visit to Palestine in the year 1898." Justifiable pride, for the Niemöllers owed the Emperor a double allegiance—he was Commander-in-Chief of the Navy and Head of the Evangelical Church in Prussia.

The Emperor's birthday was on 27 January. In Germany it

was a public holiday and the occasion was duly celebrated on board the *Hertha*, then in Genoa. German citizens from the town attended church on board, the ship was dressed overall and in the evening the German Club gave a dinner and dance at the Hotel Miramare. Despite the excitement, however, Niemöller did not forget to look up an old friend of the family, the minister Rostan Calvino. This man was a member of the Waldensian sect, so called because it had been founded by Petrus Waldus, a merchant of Lyons, in about the year 1200. The Waldensians did not observe the sacraments and they strictly abjured a priesthood. Throughout the Middle Ages they suffered periodic persecution, and in course of time the members of the sect scattered from their original home in the South of France, some of them settling in southern Germany where they were partially absorbed into the Protestant Church. Some may still be found in the United States and Italy. Niemöller's liking for the Waldensians, whom he frequently visited in later years and whose invitations to preach he has always gladly accepted, dates perhaps from this time.

Meanwhile the Emperor's birthday had offered plenty of excitement, but it stirred no profound emotion, none of that semi-mystical fervour that the distant sight of William II had inspired a few months previously. They had had a chance encounter on the high seas with the famous Imperial yacht, *Hohenzollern*. While the band of the *Hertha* played the Imperial Anthem, she dipped her ensign, fired a salute of thirty-three guns, and the cadets mustered with the remainder of the ship's company on deck had caught a glimpse of a small figure standing motionless in the wing of the *Hohenzollern's* bridge, and as the gleaming yacht slid past—white from stem to stern—a gloved hand came up to the salute—the Emperor's hand, acknowledging the *Hertha's* loyal greetings. . . . A moment to remember, a moment that somehow paid for many months of boat-pulling, watch-keeping, and the rest.

The *Hertha* had reached Venice in time for Christmas Day,

and to the Pimples, most of whom had never before spent Christmas away from home, that was an unforgettable experience, too. The upper deck was dressed with flags and an altar was set up in front of the ship's bell flanked on either side with Christmas trees. After Divisions came church and after church they had opened their Christmas mail. Then they had gone ashore— stared and been stared at—made notes about St. Mark's Square and the Doge's Palace for their logs—and returned to sing *Stille Nacht, heilige Nacht* and *Tannenbaum*. Thereafter their memories of the day became a little confused. The singing had been in the wardroom. Some time later the Pimples had forgathered in their own mess, the gunroom, and drank Chianti. There were no midshipmen on board and the Sub-Lieutenant who was normally in charge of them was the guest of the Captain, so the Pimples were alone. Oh! That Chianti. . . ! Towards midnight, the din was terrific. Some of them were trying to play hockey on the mess table. Then suddenly the door had opened and the First Lieutenant was standing there, pale and angry, wearing a greatcoat over his pyjamas. His cabin was immediately below the gunroom. He had not had a wink of sleep and he told the Pimples to "pipe down" in no uncertain terms. Next day, Number One had still been feeling sore and had reported the cadets' behaviour to the Captain. The Captain had gazed at them long and steadily and some of them were just beginning to feel a curious shifting sensation in the pit of the stomach, when the Old Man had said quietly: "Next time you give a party, gentlemen, what about inviting me?"

All this, of course, was "off the record"—not the sort of thing to put in the log. But Cadet Niemöller faithfully recorded the events of that Christmas Day in a letter to his younger brother, Wilhelm, who also fancied a naval career. The log itself remained severely nautical in tone. No poetic descriptions, no pen pictures—nothing but facts, figures and the occasional painstakingly accurate illustration of a ship or a piece of equipment. However, the cadets had to be encouraged to develop their powers of observation, and the natural features of a coast-line as seen from the ship, major towns, river estuaries, et cetera, required mention in the log, if only to convince the training officer that the cadets had kept their eyes open. Maybe it casts no reflection on the youthful Niemöller's imaginative powers, therefore, when we find Tangier, which presents a startlingly attractive sight from the sea, described as follows: "the town lies picturesquely on a somewhat steep elevation"; mountains, as "forbidding and jagged"; the coast-line of Norway, as "like stage scenery, dwarfing the ship". A more ambitious attempt to describe the scene would certainly have been thought out of place.

The purpose of keeping a log, as of all else in the cadets' training programme, was to assist them to become efficient naval officers—and that meant in war as well as in peace. Prose poems were irrelevant. When, therefore, we come across an entry in Cadet Niemöller's log that does betray sentiment or an appreciation of nature, it is safe to conclude that his feelings are revealed despite his efforts to restrain them. When the cadets went ashore at Plymouth, for example, he wrote: "the scenery here has a strange suggestion of home about it"—which meant, probably, that he was overwhelmed by nostalgia for the green fields of his native Westphalia. He had already learnt to love the English landscape two years before, when he had visited Windsor and Richmond. Westphalia was the standard by which he compared everything he saw. "In some ways Bornholm reminds me of my Westphalian home," states the log after Niemöller had visited the island. The inhabitants of Skagen, in Denmark, with their "fresh, cheerful, healthy faces" also reminded him of the Westphalians, while the inhabitants of industrial Göteborg summoned visions of the pale, peevish faces he saw in his father's parish of Elberfeld. Finally, a visit which the cadets paid to the famous red-brick Gothic castle of Marienburg in West Prussia prompted further Westphalian analogies. "The first thing that struck me," stated Niemöller, "was that red brick can be used in other buildings besides railway stations in Westphalia. . . ."

These entries in the log are exceptional. The vast majority keep strictly to naval matters. If the young cadets had acquired any special cultural interests at school, they were not encouraged to pursue them on board *Hertha*, and the relentless training programme left them no time to do so. Cadet Niemöller had been given a classical education; the sight of Mount Etna as they steamed past Sicily prompted the quick note: "In this part of the Mediterranean the battle was fought out between Greek culture and that of Carthage—but we have no time for such thoughts." It was not the past, but the present with which young Germans of 1910 were concerned.

Understandably enough, pride in all things German sometimes led to intolerance of everything not German. "Odde, or in Norwegian, Odda, is a minute little place distinguished, firstly, by two fair-sized hotels and, secondly, by a carbide factory that poisons the entire atmosphere. . . ." So much for Odde. Concerning the Sea of Marmara, the log states: "What an anchorage! But no harbour facilities, no industry, etc. Strange how the most incompetent nations are the ones most richly endowed by Nature! What would not Germany give for such a harbour!" When Swedish officials objected to the *Hertha's* longboat coming too close to some fortifications, the log contemptuously accuses them of "persecution mania". The French battleship *Henri IV* encountered in Bizerta Harbour is dismissed as "certainly the ugliest ship to have been built in modern times." On examining the British dockyard at Plymouth, Cadet Niemöller misses "that orderliness which makes it so easy to find one's way around our own dockyards." The cleanliness of the Yugoslav port of Kotor, on the other hand, is not credited to the Yugoslavs, but by a curious process of thought, is ascribed to traces "even here of German thoroughness and order". A bull-fight which young Niemöller attended in Spain is judged from a rather self-conscious standpoint. "By no means so unpleasant as to force a cultivated European to swoon, bull-fighting is clearly an art requiring considerable courage and skill, but the goring of defenceless horses by the bull is cruel and, to our way of feeling, repellent."

*   *   *

The training cruise ended in March, 1911, when the *Hertha* returned to Kiel. Martin Niemöller had been exactly one year in the Imperial Navy. From Kiel he travelled on leave to Elberfeld, where his school friend, Hermann Bremer, was waiting at the station to meet him. After a few enjoyable days at home distributing souvenirs of the cruise and being generally fêted, Martin set off on a tour of his other Westphalian relations. Throughout his leave he kept up his log, noting events with the most meticulous accuracy. Visits to the Bremer family were numerous. Besides Hermann, who was to be killed as a U-boat officer in the First World War, there was his brother, Fritz, who later became a doctor, and his sister, Else—one day to be Martin Niemöller's wife.

The first year in the navy ended with the promotion exam to Midshipman. After passing this test, in which fifteen per cent of the examinees usually failed, Niemöller was then faced with a further and more specialized examination which included papers on navigation, mathematics, physics, chemistry, tactics and ship construction. This test took place after another year's training, again at the Flensburg-Mürwik Training School on the borders of Denmark. In March, 1912, Niemöller successfully cleared this hurdle, and from then on was entitled to wear the Midshipman's dirk and bear the additional title of Ensign. He could be well satisfied with his progress, particularly as his had been the best papers in the exam. Thereafter, in the summer of 1912, came a number of specialist courses which Niemöller described in retrospect as amounting to "a semi-permanent state of C.B.". They included a whole month of infantry training in Wilhelmshaven and the army training area on Lüneburg Heath, eight weeks at the Torpedo School in Mürwik, and three months at the School of Gunnery in Sonderburg. As a final agony, the trainees then performed a 20-mile route-march in full kit, starting at 9 p.m. and ending at 3 a.m. Then they had half-an-hour —no more, no less—in which to change and pack their belongings, and from 3.30 until 7 a.m. there was a farewell party flowing with wine and ribaldry.

One hundred and eighty midshipmen emerged, relieved but exhausted, from their over-organized life in barracks with but a single wish—to get to sea again as quickly as possible. Each man was allowed to state his preference before being posted to a ship, and, encouraged by his good exam results to think that his request might conceivably be granted, Niemöller asked to serve in the Far Eastern Squadron. The cruise of the *Hertha* had whetted his appetite for strange lands and peoples. But it was to remain unsatisfied. To his great disgust, he and twelve other midshipmen were appointed to the 23,000-ton battleship *Thüringen* which, as part of the North Sea Fleet, was stationed in Wilhelmshaven. But Niemöller was lucky. No sooner had he joined the ship than he was selected to become torpedo officer. This entailed a second course in torpedoes at the Mürwik Training School, and it was the spring of 1913 before Niemöller saw the *Thüringen* again, this time to join her as a Sub-Lieutenant with the appointment of Second Torpedo Officer. He was also detailed to watch over the welfare of the twelve Midshipmen who had formerly been his colleagues. He took them in P.T. and, as "target officer", was in charge of them during practice shoots when a tug trailed a string of 50-foot pontoons for them to fire at. All this Niemöller found pleasant enough. At last he could call himself a responsible naval officer. Gone were the days of "Pimples", "Warts" and "Snotties". The worst that slang could muster for him now was "Sub", and that was a term of endearment almost. At least he was no longer an "excrescence".

The outbreak of war on 4 August, 1914, found the battleship

Thüringen cruising in the North Sea. The officers were eager to come to grips with the enemy. Instead, for a whole year—while on land the German armies advanced to within reach of victory—the nearest that Niemöller and his fellow officers ever got to the fighting was an occasional raid on the British coast, an attack in the Gulf of Riga and battle-practice interspersed with athletic meetings complete with prizes and tea-tents. After these diversions "the good old *Thüringen*" withdrew to permanent safety in Wilhelmshaven and the junior officers had perforce to restrain their warlike ardour in long spells of watch-keeping dressed in peace-time rig, including sword-belt. Meanwhile, as Niemöller records in his autobiography, "we dreamt of torpedo-boats, airships, and submarines . . . nothing served to allay the growing boredom . . . people began to lose their sense of humour, so much so that some of the older batchelors could find nothing better to do than bow their necks under the yoke of matrimony. . . ."

The younger officers did all they could to get transferred to more active employment and in October, 1915, as a result of his efforts or his excellent service record, Niemöller was summoned by the Captain and informed that he was to transfer to the U-boat Branch on 1 December. When it came to the point, he felt a pang of regret at leaving the *Thüringen*, sensing perhaps that the carefree days of his youth were now over and that he stood on the brink of adult responsibilities. The journey to Kiel, the U-boat headquarters, was, indeed, a journey into the unknown. At best, thought Niemöller, he would be sent on yet another course, this time a watch-keepers' course in the S/M Training School. At worst, he would find himself doing barrack duty in Kiel-Wik with U-boat trainees. In the event, he got something in between, and was sent to the U-boat depot-ship *Vulkan* as a watch-keeper. Fortunately that did not last long. On 1 January, 1916, he was sent on a W/T course, and six weeks later he was entering the last stage of his training before becoming a fully fledged U-boat officer.

Niemöller was still struggling to master the intricacies of venting and flooding, "putting on the trim", diving and surfacing, at the U-boat Training School at Eckernförde, when an urgent request for replacements was received by wireless from a U-boat homeward bound in the North Sea. The boat was the U.73, a big mine-laying U-boat that had been only recently commissioned. In heavy weather with a following sea the entire bridge-watch of four men had been swept overboard. The news reached the training school on 22 February. Twenty-four hours later, Niemöller was on his way to Kiel to join the U.73 in place of the officer who had been drowned. On the 24th, the U.73 duly tied up in Kiel. When the Commander saw his new watch-keeping officer waiting on the quayside, bag in hand and ready to come aboard, he looked far from pleased. "How do you know I'm prepared to have you?" he said. "As I did not know," records Niemöller, "there was little I could say." However, when the Commander learned that Niemöller was a torpedo specialist and had also completed his W/T course, he began to thaw. To expect an experienced watch-keeper was too much to ask in those early days of the war. He magnanimously decided to give Niemöller a trial—and they sailed happily together for the rest of that year.

But first, the U.73 had to spend several weeks in the dockyard having the extensive damage repaired that she had suffered in the North Sea storms. Added to this disappointment, came the sober realization that the U.73 was by no means an ideal fighting machine. Far from it. The maximum surface speed the two Koerting Diesel engines could muster was $9\frac{1}{2}$ knots, while submerged the most that could be hoped for was an occasional fifteen-minute "burst" of 4 knots. Diving—if all went well, as it seldom did—took at least two minutes, and surfacing, owing to the fact that the diving tanks had to be blown with the bilge-pump, was anybody's guess. It would be an amazing fluke, therefore, if the gallant vessel ever came within torpedo range of an enemy ship. As for the only alternative, namely sinking by gun-fire, the designers had thoughtfully mounted the 3·5-inch gun abaft the conning tower, so that, unless the Commander decided to sacrifice further bridge parties, the U-boat would have to be steered beam-on or stern-on to the target. The fact was, as Niemöller discovered, that the boat was designed for mine-laying, not fighting.

The Commanding Officer, *Kapitänleutnant* Siess, was not the man, however, to accept an entirely passive role and during the refit he went to Berlin to see what the German Admiralty had to offer him in the way of excitement. He came back with a heavily sealed envelope full of secret instructions. As they could get nothing out of him, his officers, meanwhile, had to content themselves with the sight of the U-boat being filled up to the last square-inch of space with food and Diesel oil. There could be only one conclusion, and having reached it, the Engineer Officer cast a dubious glance at his engines. "*I* don't mind, so long as these sewing machines don't."

On 1 April, 1916, after embarking thirty-four mines at Cuxhaven, the U.73 sailed past Heligoland, heading for the open sea. When the last link with home had dropped below the horizon, the Commander let his men into the secret: they were going to mine the enemy's shipping lanes and harbour entrances in the Mediterranean.

* * *

The weather in the Heligoland Bight was tolerably good, but as they crossed the North Sea, heading towards the Shetland Islands, the wind steadily increased and they began to meet mountainous seas. The old hands nodded sagely and talked about April being a tricky month in those parts. Those who, like Niemöller were experiencing their first ocean-going patrol felt that "tricky" was something of an understatement: the U.73 was revealing yet more of her vices, wallowing like some great, helpless whale in the troughs of the waves until half the ship's company were longing only to die. From time to time, the U-boat would give a sudden lurch and wrench lockers from their fixings against the bulkheads. Splintered wood and the men's personal belongings became scattered about until the inside of the hull began to look like a rubbish dump.

After they had rounded the Shetlands and altered course westwards, they ran into a north-westerly gale and the sea became a foaming cauldron. The men of the bridge-watch had to be lashed to the rails. The gyro-compass packed up and for a time, there being no stars visible, they had to navigate by dead reckoning. The galley was unusable, but no one was hungry— except the first watch-keeping officer, whom Niemöller saw one morning avidly consuming a thick slice of black bread spread with butter and tinned liver-sausage reinforced with a layer of jam, and topped with mixed pickles. . . .

After ten days they had passed the south-west point of Ireland and were heading for the Bay of Biscay. Here they had their first encounter with the enemy, sinking a large British sailing ship by gun-fire after its crew had taken to the boats. But in the process one of the bridge-watch had been lost overboard and no one felt inclined to celebrate the success. The weather was improving and during the following night the U.73 laid twelve mines in the entrance to Lisbon Harbour, making off westwards after completion of the task under cover of darkness. Next morning, when they surfaced, they found themselves in the middle of a Portuguese fishing fleet, peacefully casting nets and lines. At the sight of the submarine, the crews broke into a babel of shouting and immediately started to row off, setting sail as they went. But the U-boat hoisted the French Tricolour—amity was restored and the secret of a German U-boat's presence so close in to Lisbon was preserved. Meanwhile the U.73 had picked up a wireless message to the effect that a 5000-ton Norwegian ship laden with wheat had struck one of the mines laid off Lisbon and foundered.

As the U.73 headed towards the Straits of Gibraltar, the weather continued to improve. On 19 April the Rock came into view. It was a lovely spring day with a gentle breeze from the north-west and a school of porpoises playing in the morning sunshine. Columns of smoke ahead showed that there was plenty of traffic in the Straits. Now that a westerly gale would have been welcome as enabling the U-boat to pass through into the Mediterranean unseen, the visibility was, of course, excellent—in fact, dangerously good! But the capacity of the batteries was too small to enable the U-boat to run the gauntlet submerged. There was nothing for it but to try their luck on the surface. All went well until about 4 p.m. when the officer of the watch reported that they were being shadowed by a British steamer on the starboard beam. The vessel was maintaining the same slow speed as the U-boat and when engine trouble caused the latter to stop, the steamer stopped, too. She now started calling up the U-boat by W/T and as it proved impossible to decode the messages, the Germans were unable to reply. With the engines restored to life, the U.73 resumed the voyage, every man on board closed up at diving stations.

In order to shake off the unwelcome escort, the Commander finally hoisted the White Ensign—whereupon the enemy ship flew the Blue Ensign, but continued to imitate the U-boat's every change of course. At about 6 p.m., when a large ship appeared on the port bow, coming from the eastward, the Commander decided it was time to submerge and accordingly, still flying the White Ensign, the U.73 was sent down to 60 feet. Two hours later, having shaken off her pursuers, she surfaced off the Spanish coast. At nightfall, the Commander tried again to pass through the Straits and this time succeeded, submerging to avoid searchlights mounted on the Rock as the U-boat slipped through the narrows.

Unfavourable weather conditions combined with technical defects in the U-boat then compelled the Commander to abandon a project for laying mines off Bizerta and head instead for Valetta, the British fleet anchorage in Malta. Despite incessant enemy patrolling and one or two serious alarms, twenty-two mines were successfully laid off the harbour entrance and the

U.73 then disengaged and headed north-east towards the Strait of Otranto. On their way the wireless picked up a British Admiralty report that the battleship H.M.S. *Russell* had struck a mine and foundered in the Mediterranean. One of theirs? It seemed probable, for some days later the British sloop H.M.S. *Nasturtium* and an armed yacht were also reported to have been mined off Malta and when the U.73 in due course safely reached Austrian territorial waters, the entire crew were decorated on the express instructions of the aged Emperor, Francis Joseph.

A fortnight later, when Niemöller reported to the Officer Commanding U-boats in Kiel he had every reason to feel pleased with his first patrol, particularly so when the officer's first words on catching sight of him were: "What! You still alive? I thought the U.73 had gone to the bottom long ago!"

In Kiel the U.73 was known as the "floating coffin"; that she should stay afloat was apparently more than anyone dared to hope. Nevertheless and despite the fact that she undoubtedly deserved the name, she and her crew continued throughout the following months to do useful work. Meanwhile, until essential repairs were completed in the dockyard at Pola, the ship's company enjoyed themselves basking in the brilliant sunshine and bathing at the "Pigeon Grotto" in the clear blue water. Now and again the officers and their Austrian friends would brew themselves a bowl of genuine punch and consume it sitting on the limestone cliffs above the grotto, returning to the ancient frigate, *Adria*, which served as depot ship, for dinner. Some of his companions Niemöller already knew from the days when the *Hertha* had visited the Adriatic on the cadets' training cruise. Now, in the midst of their idyll, news reached them of the Battle of Jutland, and with it the recollection that they themselves were merely resting between battles.

At last the day came when the U.73 was pronounced ready for sea—as ready as she would ever be—and after some cautious diving tests during which everything worked more or less normally, she sailed once more for patrol. Once more, mines were laid and ships sunk, this time off Salonika, in the Gulf of Orfano, near the Greek island of Phlebes, and off Port Said and Alexandria. On returning to Pola the men heard that in all, their mines had accounted for close on 100,000 tons of enemy shipping, and, as Niemöller writes in his autobiography: "we had known of no success beyond the pitiful Greek barque *Propontis*. But we now learned that our minefield in the Kea Channel had bagged the British hospital ship, *Britannic*, a magnificent vessel of nearly 50,000 tons, the pride of the British mercantile marine . . . the 'floating coffin' was beginning to pay her way. . . ."

During those months, the German U-boat flotilla in the Mediterranean had been strongly reinforced. The U.72 a sister-ship of the U.73 arrived safely, a number of smaller but faster mine-laying boats belonging to the U.C.-class and three of the latest torpedo-carrying U-boats designed for long-range patrol work. Meanwhile, the U.73 was at sea again with orders to lay mines off Port Said and Alexandria and destroy shipping in that area. On 21 December they sighted a large tanker escorted by a trawler. After a long pursuit and intricate manœuvring, the Commander succeeded in putting one torpedo into the tanker which slowly capsized after the trawler had taken off the crew. On board the U-boat the victory was celebrated with *Deutschland über alles* on the gramophone.

Next day the last mines were laid off Alexandria and then the U-boat turned her nose towards the Adriatic and home. But with one torpedo remaining on board, it was still the Commander's duty to contact enemy shipping. On the morning of 23 December they encountered a medium-sized liner and were preparing to attack when they saw she was a neutral, the Dutch ship *Rembrandt*. The Commander went in closer and the men on the bridge watched the passengers walking about on the promenade deck. The sight of this oasis of peace and comfort in the midst of war aroused the bitter envy of the U-boat men, until they realized that the people they saw were living in false security: at any time the liner might strike a mine and they themselves fall victim to the scourge that involved every nation in Europe. "Indeed, no one could stand aside, there was no one to be envied," wrote Niemöller later. "We ourselves had to go on and would go on until the war was at an end or we were stopped by superior force. And how soon that would be, who could say?"

In the early hours of Christmas Eve, while the U-boat was labouring through high seas within sight of Crete, the port propeller shaft broke. Soon after, the air induction to the one remaining Diesel engine developed a fault. While the engine-room staff sweated to repair the damage, the Commander managed to maintain steerage way on the starboard electric motor. Meanwhile, Niemöller sat on his bunk reading the Gospel for Christmas Day in his Confirmation Bible. As he was doing so, the boatswain's mate came through the bulkhead bearing a minute Christmas tree made out of matchwood, green straw and red-tipped pins. "It's Christmas, sir," he said, and put the tree down on the chart table in front of Niemöller.

At 10 p.m. the starboard engine was got going again and the U-boat began to limp slowly ahead. Then it was discovered that sea-water was leaking into one of the cylinders via the water-cooling jacket. To repair the jacket required welding equipment and that was available only in the dockyard. There was nothing for it, therefore, but to keep over-lubricating the bearings in the hope that the engine would not seize up, and Christmas Day was chiefly notable for the fact that 270 gallons of lubricating oil were consumed within 24 hours. After further delays, repairs and breakdowns, the U.73 reached the Strait of Otranto on the night of 28 December. She passed through unmolested and finally reached base in time for the crew to celebrate the New Year in something like civilized surroundings.

But the days of the U.73 were numbered. She took part in one operation off the Syrian coast in 1918 and then in October of that year her crew scuttled her to prevent her falling into the hands of the Italians. Meanwhile, throughout the year 1917, the "coffin" was unfit even to deserve the adjective "floating." Niemöller was too junior to get a command of his own. He would first have to put in another six months as watch-keeping officer, but where, and with whom? As luck would have it, on New Year's Eve Niemöller learned that the Commander of the U.39 was looking for a navigating warrant officer. His own had broken an arm on patrol and time was short—the boat was due to sail again on 3 January. Knowing that warrant officers with experience of navigation were rarer than gold, Niemöller persuaded his own Commander to allow him to volunteer for the job and reluctantly the latter agreed. On New Year's Day, Niemöller was accepted and by evening his gear was transferred and he was *de facto*—and who cared whether *de jure!*—a member of the ship's company of the U.39.

The U.39 sailed for patrol on the afternoon of 3 January, 1917. By comparison with the old U.73 she was a submariner's dream. First of all—a fighting U-boat: no mines, only torpedoes. Then, her speed: she could do 13 knots quite easily. Finally, and most important of all from the point of view of success: officers and men were seasoned in battle and got on well together. In less than a week the first enemy ship was sighted. The torpedo struck home and she sank rapidly. Then the chase began. In the preceding months the enemy had learned valuable lessons and they now had quite a number of devices to make life more dangerous for a U-boat, besides introducing the convoy system which made it harder to reach a target. The enemy warships were now equipped with hydrophones, for instance, for picking up the sound of a U-boat's engines when she was underwater. Their depth-charges were much more deadly than the old-time "crackers," and once a U-boat had made its appearance in a certain area, the enemy re-routed his entire sea traffic until the area was clear again. This last factor was the one which caused trouble to the U.39. For days after the initial success not a single enemy ship was sighted with the exception of one collier, and that only because she carried no wireless. The weather was cold and rainy, visibility was down to three or four miles. Where were the ships? Every day, morning and evening, the same question—unanswered. Finally the Commander decided to head for the nearest enemy port.

Meanwhile, as navigating officer with hardly any practical experience of navigation, Niemöller was too busy with his own problems to worry much about the enemy. "At dawn, I worked out our position from the stars. During the forenoon, I fixed our position by the sun, then I took the noon sight. In the afternoon, I shot the sun again, then in the evening, took a star sight again —provided the weather was right. In the intervals I had to plot our course and log all alterations of course and speed . . . it was all very interesting and instructive, but of course the U-boat was not on patrol solely for the purpose of teaching me navigation!"

On reaching Alexandria in poor visibility, the U.39 still could find no trace of enemy shipping. For a whole day, the U-boat lay hove-to while the ship's company took it in turns to bathe in the open sea. That, believed the Commander, should surely tempt Fate into bringing a whole flotilla of warships on to the scene. But apart from a lone collier torpedoed on the following day, the seas remained without a trace of friend or foe. So they moved north-westwards towards the Ionian Sea and the route normally used by British troop transports making for Salonika. For days they hovered about on latitude 36° N., the same latitude that bisects the island of Malta, while the weather steadily deteriorated. Still no sign of a ship! The engineer officer was meanwhile getting worried about the state of the batteries and when he asked the Commander to return to base as they were in urgent need of overhaul, the latter readily agreed.

On 25 January, when the U-boat was heading northwards, two columns of smoke were sighted on the western horizon. Altering course towards them, the Commander identified two ships escorted by no less than three modern French destroyers. Standing beside him in the conning-tower, Niemöller watched the Commander carry out the attack. For his work on previous patrols, the latter had already been awarded the highest decoration, the German equivalent to the V.C., the *Pour le Mérite*. After a lot of manœuvring at periscope depth, the torpedo sight was just coming on to the target. Sixty yards away a destroyer had just crossed the U-boat's bow. "Slow ahead together!" A glance at the torpedo sight mounted on the periscope shaft. Four more degrees to go.

"A troopship!" said the Commander, eyes glued to the lens. "Fo'c'sle full of men. Up periscope!"

"Here she comes. . . . No. 1 tube. . . . stand by. . . ."

With his cap pushed to the back of his head, the Commander paused, then, still gazing through the periscope, said quietly: "Fire." Then immediately: "Down periscope. Deep! 100 feet!"

On the order to dive, the Commander, followed by Niemöller, clattered down into the control-room where the men standing at the flooding valves had already spun them open. The water boomed into the tanks. The next second as the operators set the hydroplanes to dive, the bow of the U-boat started to drop and the men clung on as the hull slanted down. The Commander was gazing at his stop-watch, timing the torpedo's run. Five seconds —ten—fifteen—and then the tension snapped as a dull roar came rolling under the sea.

Ten minutes later, the Commander came to periscope-depth again to take a look at the target. The troopship was sinking stern-first with one destroyer standing by, picking up survivors. The second troopship with the remaining two destroyers were making off at high speed. In his autobiography Niemöller described the dilemma with which the Commander was now faced:

"What should we do? We did not want to interrupt the work of saving lives—few enough would be saved as it was. On the other hand, the men being fished out of the water were soldiers destined to fight against German troops. . . . We tried to get off a second torpedo, but before we could get the sights on, the destroyer spotted us and let fly a hail of shells. They missed, because all they could see of us was our periscope, but it meant the attack was off. All we could do was to move around raising and lowering our periscope occasionally so as to prevent the destroyer concentrating on the rescue work. Then, when the troopship had finally disappeared, we left the scene and started for home."

War was war, or so they had told themselves at the time, but later as they were sailing home, the officers could not help asking themselves whether their action in trying to stop the rescue work could be justified. Lengthy discussions developed in the wardroom, and gradually "the whole complex problem of war presented itself to us and we realized from this single experience of ours something of the tragedy involved . . . we saw that situations could arise in war in which it was utterly impossible to preserve a clear conscience. Assuming we survived, the question of whether our conscience survived with us depended on whether we believed in the forgiveness of sins." War, in fact, made sin inevitable: war *was* sin. "That 25 January," concluded Niemöller, "was the turning point of my life, because it opened my eyes to the utter impossibility of a moral universe."

At the time, however, the operational hazards of passing through the Strait of Otranto soon dimmed the memory of the questionable incident and thereafter, when the U.39 had successfully reached base, the conferment of the Iron Cross First Class helped for the moment to reduce inner doubts to manageable proportions.

* * *

Niemöller's old boat, the U.73, had meanwhile been laid up as unseaworthy and he was therefore absolved from the grim necessity of reporting back for duty in the "floating coffin." He was given a good spell of home leave after which he hoped to be sent on a Commanding Officer's Course at U-boat Headquarters. Instead, he was ordered to report to Tondern on the borders of Denmark, for special training in the deciphering of intercepted enemy wireless messages. Though he had his suspicions that someone had made a mistake, he went—and found himself in the company of expert mathematicians. In a sudden access of humility, Niemöller decided that they could safely be left to do the deciphering while he made off to explore the naval airships which, luckily, were based on Tondern. As a U-boat officer he could plead that a fortnight spent in becoming acquainted with airships and aircraft was infinitely more useful than grappling all day with glorified crossword puzzles.

Before long, Niemöller was on good terms with the officer commanding the naval Zeppelin, L.23, and to him he owed one of his finest wartime adventures—an 18-hour reconnaissance flight over shipping routes between Scotland and Norway. His appetite for flying now thoroughly aroused, Niemöller decided it was time he went up in an aeroplane and there, too, his personal contacts brought about the desired result—or rather, a part of it. For the intention was that the instructor of the flying school should take him up in a two-seater plane; instead of which, Niemöller found himself sitting behind a pupil while the latter performed his first solo flight.

Reporting to the Admiralty in Berlin after his intensive deciphering course, Niemöller then found himself detailed for a desk-job in the Mediterranean Section. "Pen-pushing" was the last thing he would have chosen to do in the fourth year of war, but the work had its compensations. It enabled him to see the daily reports from General Ludendorff's Army Headquarters and hence provided him with a true picture of the war situation and, in the personal sphere, it enabled him to renew acquaintance with the girl he was ultimately to marry. This was the eldest sister of his school friend, Hermann Bremer. Else Bremer was studying at that time in Berlin and after a chance encounter, she and Martin Niemöller spent their free Sunday afternoons sailing on the Wannsee. Neither of them had many friends in Berlin. The spring days were warm and sunny, ideal for outings in the surrounding countryside, and a friendship quickly developed which, a year later, resulted in their engagement.

Meanwhile, Niemöller's spell at the Admiralty had ended as suddenly as it had begun and he was once more appointed to sea-going service, this time in a large, ocean-going U-boat with a complement of eighty. The U.151 had just completed her trials and this was to be her first patrol. For four months, from September until Christmas, 1917, she waged war on Atlantic shipping with Niemöller as her First Lieutenant. On the way out, via the Shetlands and the west coast of Ireland, the Commander was well and truly hoodwinked by a British Q-ship—an innocent looking merchant vessel with a concealed armament of guns served by naval gunners. Having torpedoed the ship, he surfaced to watch her sink, and had his own gun and most of the bridge reduced to scrap. Fortunately for the U-boat, she was still able to dive, though in the process she shipped several tons of water through a jammed conning-tower hatch.

After herculean efforts by the fitters and riveters among the crew the damage was patched up and the U.151 "proceeded," though now with a limp. Heading down into the Bay of Biscay, they encountered fine autumn weather and seas like glass. For a few days, war seemed remote. At sundown the members of the off-duty watch were allowed up on to the after casing for a smoke and a breath of air. Someone produced an accordion and that strange admixture of romanticism and melancholy that lies at the bottom of many German songs would not be denied:

> *Ich weiss nicht, was soll es bedeuten,*
> *Dass ich so traurig bin;*
> *Ein Märchen aus alten Zeiten,*
> *Das kommt mir nicht aus dem Sinn.*
>
> *Die Luft ist kühl und es dunkelt,*
> *Und ruhig fliesst der Rhein;*
> *Der Gipfel des Berges funkelt*
> *Im Abendsonnenschein. . . .*

"The air is cool and it darkens, and quietly flows the

Rhine . . ." Memories stirred and their thoughts turned to their loved ones at home—home, in Germany—Germany, bleeding, dying, but fighting on . . . As the moon rose, huge and limpid over the silken bosom of the sea, the concert ended, and the men roared out their battle-song: "*Denn wir fahren—denn wir fahren—gegen Engel-land!*"

Biscay, Cape Finisterre, Madeira, the Canary Islands, Dakar, Porto Grande—it proved to be a long patrol, the longest of any German U-boat in the First World War: 114 days at sea, covering an average daily distance of 100 miles. In that time they destroyed about 50,000 tons of enemy shipping—nine merchant ships, five sailing ships and one destroyer. The destroyer nearly took the U.151 with her. It was on the night of 11 October. The U-boat was submerged at 100 feet. The Commander was in the control-room, but his First Lieutenant had turned in. Suddenly Niemöller found himself awake and rolling on the floor. A violent shock had thrown him clean out of his bunk. Fearing the worst, he ran down the gangway to the control-room. The Commander was in the conning-tower. He must have gone to periscope depth while Niemöller was asleep. He was just lowering the periscope. "Yes," he said calmly when he saw his Number One, "we have been rammed. . . ." At that moment there was a terrific explosion and the lights went out. Thinking it was a depth-charge, the Commander dived to 200 feet and then awaited the next. But none came. . . .

"Forty feet! Up periscope!" A quick all-round look through the lens—nothing in sight. Thirty feet—twenty-five feet: another look—still all clear. "Surface!" The Commander pushed open the upper lid and climbed out on to the bridge, followed by Number One. There, right across the stern, gaped a 13-foot hole.

Two days later, after frenzied repairs during which they discovered that the pressure-hull was mercifully still intact, a W/T signal was intercepted stating than an American destroyer was reported missing in European waters. The Commander pieced together the rest of the story. He had come to periscope depth and was taking a first all-round sweep through the lens. As he looked aft, he saw a vast grey wall—the next instant the destroyer rammed. Parts of a propeller were discovered embedded in the U-boat's deck and from the underwater explosion, it was judged that the destroyer had torn her bottom off as she passed overhead with the result that the boilers exploded and she sank like a stone.

From the enemy merchant ships encountered, the Commander took whatever they needed in the U.151—lubricating oil, food, coffee, beer, copper, rubber, soap, clothing—on one occasion, even some cases of ladies' silk stockings were hauled on board and distributed among the crew to give as presents on their return home. Before long the U-boat began to look like a grocer's shop. Every square inch of space that was not taken up with loot was needed for accommodation, for gradually the numbers of prisoners-of-war on board had increased to nearly a hundred—twenty more than the entire ship's company. As long as they remained in the U-boat her fighting efficiency was seriously impaired and in due course the Commander landed the shipwrecked seamen at the Azores.

The last ship from which they were able to restock the larder was the *Margaret Roberts*, an American three-masted schooner encountered off the Straits of Gibraltar. The schooner was stopped with a warning shot over her bows and a boarding party under the command of the First Lieutenant went over from the U-boat. On examining the chart-room, Niemöller found the place littered with empty brandy bottles—and yet American ships were supposed to be "dry." The position which the master had marked on his chart that morning was inaccurate to the extent of about fifty miles, and no wonder, considering the amount of liquor the man had consumed. But Niemöller found he was a decent fellow and gave him the benefit of the doubt: the brandy, of course, had been purely for medicinal purposes, in order to ward off the 'flu. At any rate, the master was duly grateful when Niemöller gave him his correct position and set his lifeboats on their course for Madeira. When the crew were all safely on their way, Niemöller and his men laid explosive charges in the hull and blew the ship's bottom out.

"I returned to the U.151 in the dinghy, tired and hungry," Niemöller recalls. "A delicious smell of cooking hovered over the U-boat and when I got down to the wardroom I found my messmates, including the Commander, in his shirt sleeves, demolishing their supper. 'Don't you bother,' said the Commander when he saw me, 'it's not worth eating!' But it was well worth eating and the sugared doughnuts made of the finest flour were lovely. . . ."

The middle of December, 1917, saw them on their way home at last. With the Shetlands safely astern, the U.151 swooped and hovered in a following sea, heading south-east. On the night of 20 December, she successfully eluded strong British patrols on the Orkney Isles–Stavanger line. Next day brought an east wind with snow and they made slow progress down the Skagerrak, finally reaching Germany on Christmas Eve. After sending a telegram to his family, Niemöller had a much-needed bath and then celebrated Christmas with his brother officers. First they attended Divine Service. The sermon was preached by the Catholic chaplain, and he chose as his text: "Glory to God in the highest; and on earth peace, goodwill towards men."

*　　*　　*

On 30 June, 1918, Martin Niemöller sailed for patrol from Pola, at the head of the Adriatic, as Commander of the U.67. A mine-laying U-boat, the U.67 had a maximum surface speed of $12\frac{1}{2}$ knots. She proved to be a splendid boat, easily manœuvrable, steady, and she dived like a duck. It was just bad luck that on that first patrol she sank only one enemy ship while she herself was nearly destroyed. Niemöller's orders were vague. He had been told simply to lay mines off Marseilles and harass shipping off the south coast of France. On 6 July, off Pantelleria, an enemy convoy was sighted sailing towards the U-boat. As it approached, Niemöller could make out twenty merchant ships with an almost equal number of escorts. Among the latter were trawlers, destroyers and a yacht flying a captive balloon.

Closing at periscope-depth, Niemöller waited until the leading escort vessel had passed him on a reciprocal course and then turned to get between the two lines of merchant ships nearest to him. At that moment, every ship in the convoy hoisted a signal. As it was hauled down a minute or two later, the ships altered course together—away from the U-boat. Niemöller was just able to get a torpedo in at the last ship before the remainder drew out of range. The torpedo struck. He heard the explosion, then dived deep to avoid the depth-charges. Creeping away underwater, Niemöller came to periscope-depth again after a mile or two and saw that the torpedoed ship had sunk. He also saw a seaplane approaching, and dived.

Two hours later, Niemöller judged it safe to come up again, and this time he surfaced. He had just taken over from the officer-of-the-watch, to allow the latter to take a sight, when he saw a black speck against the sun. "Control-room! DIVE! DIVE! DIVE!" Down went the men of the bridge-watch into the conning-tower and the water was flooding the diving tanks when the U-boat received three direct hits in quick succession from the seaplane's bombs. One landed close by the conning-tower flinging Niemöller off his feet. He jumped down the ladder, slamming the conning-tower hatch after him. As the boat continued to submerge, a thick stream of water started pouring through a hole torn in the hatch-cover.

To surface again would be suicide. As Niemöller dived the boat to 65 feet, then to 90 feet, then deeper still to 130 feet, two men succeeded in plugging the hole in the conning-tower hatch and the pressure of sea-water sealed the engine-room hatch tight shut: the first bomb had blown it open and a huge volume of water had already got into the hull making the boat excessively heavy. Some hours later, Niemöller ordered the boat to periscope depth, but the periscope had jammed and could not be raised. The spare periscope was then raised, but the lens had been smashed. The U-boat was blind. There was nothing for it, they would have to stay submerged until nightfall and then bring the U-boat straight to the surface, trusting to luck.

It was in such circumstances—when the fate of the whole ship's company hung in the balance and the hours slowly ticked by—that the eternal questions of life, death and human destiny would rise in Niemöller's mind. Was there a God? Was there a purpose in life? "These questions were not prompted by curiosity; they were there, facing us, demanding an answer, whether we welcomed them or not. And all we knew was, we had no answer; we could not find it."

*   *   *

Niemöller's first patrol in command of a U-boat had lasted eight days, but it was eight weeks before the U.67 could leave the dockyard in Pola. Meanwhile there was nothing Niemöller could do to hasten her repairs, and when his ship's company had gone on leave he decided to follow their example. In these, the concluding stages of the war, when the German armies were evacuating Belgium to shorten their lines and they were everywhere on the defensive, Niemöller felt the need for action. The future of Germany weighed on his mind. Though in sober calculation every single factor pointed to defeat, he could not bring himself even to imagine the possibility of anything but a tolerable settlement based on compromise. For, as he writes in his autobiography, "life is not merely a matter of planning on the basis of ascertainable fact; to be alive means to dare and to have faith".

Niemöller continues: "When I now went on leave, therefore, to Berlin via Vienna, it was not with the object of reporting to the Admiralty but in order to obtain the promised 'yes' from the girl I loved." Having obtained it, Niemöller travelled to Elberfeld to see his parents and future parents-in-law and then his engagement to Else Bremer was formally announced.

At the end of August Niemöller sailed for his second patrol in command of the U.67, again to lay mines off Marseilles and sink enemy shipping off the south of France. This time, his own skill allied to good luck enabled the tasks to be carried out without hitch or hindrance and after exactly one month at sea, Niemöller was able to report: "U.67. Mine-laying task completed. Three ships sunk, total 17,000 tons." Then on the way back to base, in the Strait of Otranto, the U-boat was suddenly attacked out of the blue by a French submarine. Niemöller and his navigating officer were on the bridge when they saw two torpedoes streaking towards the U-boat about two hundred yards away.

At full speed and with helm hard over, they waited, knowing that the orders had been given too late. The torpedoes were running just below the surface—and the first passed ahead, immediately followed by a crash as the second struck the U-boat squarely amidships—but no explosion. They were alive still, and the reason? On the opposite side of the U-boat they saw the same torpedo come to the surface for a moment, then break in two, and sink. A dud.

Astern of them the periscope of the enemy submarine was rising like a hand reaching out of the water—higher and higher. Niemöller ordered the gun crew on deck, but before they could engage, the Frenchman went down again until only the tip of his periscope showed, pointing like a minatory finger, whereupon, writes Niemöller: ". . . we made off at full speed, marvelling at our luck. . . ."

Chapter Three

MARRIAGE AND THE MINISTRY

(1918–23)

O N 29 October, 1918, Martin Niemöller sailed for the last time as a U-boat Commander. All U-boats at the Austrian naval base of Pola had been ordered to return forthwith to Germany. Six of them were found to be unseaworthy and had to be scuttled, among them the U.73 in which Niemöller had sailed on his first Mediterranean patrol over two years before.

On Niemöller's last evening in Pola, four young Austrian naval officers came on board to ask him for a passage to Germany. Mutinies had already broken out in some Austrian warships and he viewed the request with suspicion. "Why don't you want to stay here?" he asked. The four young Austrians replied that they did not want to surrender; they wanted to go on fighting for Germany. Touched though he was by this unexpected reply Niemöller had to refuse; the U-boat was already overloaded and he could not risk taking four more men with their baggage.

The voyage to Kiel took up almost the whole of November. In cold, squally weather, Niemöller steered southwards through the Adriatic, heading for the Strait of Otranto. At times visibility was almost zero and it was not until he saw the lights on Fano Island that he realized he had passed through the Strait, not to westward, as he had intended, but through the mine-infested waters north of Corfu. It seemed a miracle that the U-boat had survived and from then on, as Niemöller wrote in his autobiography: "I felt certain that some new task awaited me.

Why otherwise should God Himself have taken over our helm?"

By the time the U.67 had reached the western end of the Mediterranean several members of the crew, including the coxswain, had succumbed to influenza and in addition to his normal duties, the Commander was having to navigate and do watch-keeping as well. Nevertheless during the night of 11 November he succeeded in passing undetected through the Straits of Gibraltar. Once more visibility was poor and thanks to a heavy rainstorm Niemöller was able to remain on the surface. Next day, when the U.67 was safely in the Atlantic, the wireless reported that Germany had sued for an armistice. The news was not unexpected for German and Allied press reports, transmitted in clear, had already supplied Niemöller and his men with a rough idea of events in Germany. They had heard of the Kaiser's abdication and flight to Holland and of the proclamation of the Republic in Munich and Berlin. Moreover they were aware that mutiny had broken out among naval personnel in Kiel. But in the U.67, as in the other ten U-boats sailing home with her to Germany, the ship's company showed no signs of disaffection and the Commander decided to continue on his course rather than seek internment in Spain.

Sailing northwards as far as the Shetlands, the U-boats then crossed the North Sea and turning south, passed through the Norwegian fiords, the Skagerrak and the Little Belt, finally reaching Kiel in thick fog on 29 November, 1918. There they were met by a torpedo-boat flying the Red Flag. The eleven U-boats were ordered to tie up alongside the Blücher Pontoon in Kiel Harbour so that Gustav Noske, the Governor of Kiel and, later, Minister of Defence, could address the ships' companies. Shortly afterwards, Noske himself came out to meet them in the C.-in-C.'s launch. Suspicious of Noske, of whom none of them had ever before heard and shocked to see a German warship flying the Red Flag, the U-boat Commanders proceeded to ignore Noske and continued to fly ensigns and paying-off pen-

A photograph taken at Elberfeld during the First World War when Niemöller, then a naval lieutenant, was on leave and visiting Else Bremer, who was to become his wife in 1919 nants as they moved slowly towards the pontoon. As soon as the U.67 had made fast, Niemöller had the crew piped on deck and in the presence of the ship's company, ordered ensign and pennant to be lowered, thereby ensuring that the U-boat would have paid off before anyone had a chance to hoist the banner of revolution.

During the weeks that followed, Niemöller watched Germany's political structure disintegrate and with it the collapse of institutions whose permanence he had at one time taken for granted. Revolted by the orgy of iconoclasm around him, he clung to the values and code of honour which his naval training had given him, refusing to appear in public in naval uniform without his officer's dirk so that he could avenge any insult to the traditions which it represented. "I had been in Kiel only a few days," he wrote in his autobiography, "when I already felt a stranger in my own country."

Meanwhile, amid the chaos of defeat, Niemöller was still a naval officer and his responsibilities as such afforded a comforting though illusory sense of continuity with the Germany he had known. Within a few days of his return to Kiel, he was given six weeks' leave which he spent with his fiancée and his parents. Soon after his return to duty, at the end of January, 1919, he was ordered by the Inspector-General of Submarines to requisition a dockyard tug and tow two U-boats to Britain where they were to be surrendered in compliance with the terms of the Armistice. Niemöller sought an immediate interview with his Commodore, the Inspector-General. The conversation that ensued is recorded in his autobiography.

" 'Sir!' said Niemöller, 'I decline to carry out this order.'
" 'Why?'
" 'Because I didn't sign the Armistice and as far as I am concerned, it is up to the people who promised these submarines to England to take them there.' "

Strangely enough, the Commodore showed neither surprise

nor anger. "All right," he said quietly. "Then I'll have to tell somebody else to do it."

After the interview, Niemöller met a brother officer who had received a similar order which he also had refused to obey, but with very different results. "You'll do what you're told," the Commodore had barked, "or else you'll leave the Service!" So he had decided to obey. Years later, when they were both civilians, Niemöller met his Commodore again. "I can tell you now," said the latter, "I was very pleased you said 'no'."

Though Niemöller was not dismissed the Service after this incident, he saw clearly that to stay on in the Navy would be to invite a repetition. At any time he might receive another order conflicting with his sense of honour which he would again be obliged to disobey, with more serious consequences, perhaps, than on the first occasion. There was no alternative, therefore, but to resign his commission. If he did so, how would he contrive to exist? In a country disunited and materially stricken, the prospects of earning a living seemed poor in the extreme.

For a while Niemöller and a number of his friends thought of emigrating to the Argentine. They planned to go with their families and settle down to a life of sheep farming. Land, as they believed, would be cheap and they could build their own houses. Niemöller's enthusiasm for the scheme fired his fiancée and throughout February and on into March, 1919, they devoted all their time to preparing for the new life overseas. Together they took Spanish lessons and contacted every possible source of information about their intended home. In Düsseldorf Niemöller came across a former Argentine sheep farmer. He went to Berlin to consult the Argentine Association and to Hamburg to seek the advice of the Spanish American Institute. A hitch in the arrangements for the emigration of himself and his friends left him undeterred, and he did nothing to encourage some well-wishers who attempted to get him a job with a Leipzig publishing firm. For some weeks the life that beckoned beyond the seas filled all his thoughts.

Then one day Niemöller received a letter from his mother's brother in Westerkappeln. Why go to the Argentine to rear sheep, wrote his uncle, when it could be done in Germany? The job could be learned on a farm in Westphalia and then Niemöller could buy one of his own with his naval savings. Meanwhile, his uncle had a friend in Tecklenburg who would be willing to take him on as an apprentice. That same day Niemöller wrote back accepting the suggestion and saying he would be ready to start work on 1 May.

First he faced the painful necessity of resigning his commission and, after the formalities were over, the still more grievous ordeal of saying good-bye to his naval friends and to the life that had been his vocation ever since, as a boy of five, he had first heard the irresistible call of the sea.

Early in April Niemöller and his former shipmates forgathered for the last time in the Skagerrak Club in Kiel. They drank and guffawed and because he was shortly to be married, they carried him round the mess in a white tablecloth—the batchelor's shroud. But it was Niemöller the sailor whom they mourned. Two days later he paid a visit to Westerkappeln to arrange the final details of his agricultural training, and then on Easter Sunday in Elberfeld he and his fiancée, Else Bremer, were married.

The possessions which tradition allowed to a newly appointed labourer were a bed and a box of personal belongings. With these loaded on to a cart behind him, Niemöller reported for work on 5 May at Wieligmann's farm near the village of Sennlich in Tecklenburg. His employer, a powerfully built man in the prime of life, set him to work at once, helping to sow oats. In the days that followed Niemöller was taught how to feed and groom horses, how to manure a field and he ploughed his first furrow. From the start he got on well with farming people and enjoyed the work, particularly in the early morning when he had to mow and bring in green fodder for the cattle. He would set out then for the pastures before sunrise, plodding with horse and cart across the silent, misted fields, returning hours later to a breakfast of hot milk porridge and hunks of black bread. The hard work in the open air, the simplicity, the routine—all helped to bring contentment to body and mind after the agonies of war and its aftermath.

There was only one snag in Niemöller's new life; there being no room for her at Wieligmann's farm, it involved living apart from his wife. At first Else stayed with his relations in the nearby town of Westerkappeln; then in Wersen, where Niemöller's father had been born, she, too, started work on a farm, learning how to rear chickens, prepare bran mashes and other animal food, tend pigs and milk cows—all the things she would have to do later when she and her husband had a farm of their own. Meanwhile they could be together only at the week-ends, from Saturday to 4.30 on Monday morning, when Niemöller set out on his bicycle to return to Wieligmann's farm.

The summer of 1919 was exceptionally fine and the autumn harvest was completed by mid-September. Then, for the first time in months, Niemöller had time to study the newspapers and see which farms were up for sale. Finding a variety to choose from he then inquired about prices—and made an unpleasant discovery. During the summer prices had risen enormously until now the small capital he had saved from his naval pay would barely buy a few acres of land, let alone a farm-house. Try as he might to devise some means of raising the necessary money, Niemöller was at last forced to admit that there were none. Yet he was determined to be his own master and, much as farming appealed to him, he could not bring himself to stay on at Wieligmann's as a farm-hand. What other careers were open to him? School-teaching might have attracted him, but that would have meant becoming an employee of the new Republican State to which he was fundamentally opposed. For some days Niemöller kept the problem of his future to himself, not intending to tell his wife that he could no longer afford to buy a farm until he could soften the blow by suggesting an alternative career.

On the evening of 17 September, his future still seemingly as blank as ever, Niemöller set out on foot for Westerkappeln to have a talk with his uncle. On the way he met the local parson and exchanged a few words with him. The encounter stirred something in his memory and as he walked on, Niemöller suddenly recalled that he had once told his school friend and shipmate, Karli Topp, that he intended to go into the Church. Why, he wondered, had the thought never recurred until now? Because the revolution that had taken place in Germany, the mutiny in the fleet, the plunge that his countrymen had taken, head first, as it seemed, and knowingly into chaos, had left Niemöller spiritually at odds with them, or, as he himself put it, "I had raised a barrier between myself and them and withdrawn behind it." Now, as he walked to Westerkappeln, he realized that while working on the land, he had recovered his sense of proportion and their common task had reunited him with his fellow-men. That night he told his wife that continually mounting prices had destroyed their hopes of farming and then, almost in the same breath, he told her of his meeting with the parson and of the memory it had revived.

Within a matter of days, Niemöller had finally made up his mind to enter the Church, though whether with the aim of becoming a theologian or the pastor of a parish he could not, at the moment, decide. Both functions seemed to have certain drawbacks. Theology in itself had never attracted him, nor did he look on it as the key to the solution of human problems. On the other hand, the mere thought of having to preach a sermon filled him with dread. Why, then, take Holy Orders? The basic reason has been described by Niemöller himself. "I had been taught as a child that belief in Christ as our Lord and Saviour and diligent attention to God's Word can transform men and give them freedom and strength. That lesson I had never forgotten, for my own experience had proved it to be true. I now became convinced that the best and most effective help I could give to my fellow countrymen in the national calamity would be to share that knowledge with them. That, I believed, would be a truer form of service than withdrawing to the depths of the country in order to farm."

Meanwhile, Niemöller had no intention of leaving his employer in the lurch. He worked on at Wieligmann's farm until the potato crop was in and then he took a day off to go to Münster where he entered his name to study theology at the university. One last morning's work at the farm, sorting potatoes and bringing in fodder for the cattle, and he said good-bye to his friends.

During that first year after the war living conditions in Germany had steadily deteriorated. The strictest rationing of fuel and foodstuffs continued and all the time prices were rising. People were beginning to live from hand to mouth. No one could plan for the future, no one could foresee how long his savings, or his salary if he had one, would suffice to keep him alive. The growing inflation combined with an explosive political atmosphere to sweep away all semblance of security. All classes of society suffered, and not least, the young men struggling to concentrate on their studies at the university. Apart from the fact that they could earn nothing except in their spare time and so were on a par financially with widows and pensioners, the atmosphere in which they were compelled to work was the exact opposite of that remote, unruffled calm traditionally associated with seats of learning. Far from being "the Islands of the Blessed", as they had once deservedly been called, the German universities were now at the very vortex of the political maelstrom. Coming fresh from the Services, the students were either fanatically right-wing traditionalists, supporting the old Imperial system and rallying under the black, white and red banner of the *Kaiserreich*, or else Democrats and Socialists paying allegiance to the black, red and gold of the Weimar Republic. These two groups, of which the first consisted largely of ex-officers who had sworn personal loyalty to the Emperor, were irreconcilably opposed, at least as far as the fanatics were concerned. Those left-wing Socialists who sincerely supported the moderate coalition government set up under the Weimar Constitution, however, shared common ground with the ex-officer students who looked on Communism as the worst of all political evils, though the latter despised the compromises of Weimar, which they nicknamed "The System".

This, briefly, was the political atmosphere at Münster University when Niemöller was admitted as a theological student early in 1920. Already he had experienced the difficulties of study peculiar to the Germany of the post-war years, having been obliged to sit for an examination in elementary Hebrew before entering the university. For ten weeks he had "crammed" under the tutorship of a pastor friend of his father's, while he and his wife stayed with his uncle in Westerkappeln. Then, shortly before Christmas, after hearing that he had passed the examination, Niemöller and his wife moved to Münster in preparation for his first term at the university. With them went all their worldly possessions: two beds, a cupboard, a table, some chairs, several large sacks of potatoes and a mountainous pile of kindling wood which Niemöller had chopped up in the intervals of studying. In Münster he and his wife had arranged to rent three attic rooms in a rectory; they were to be their home for the next five years.

When the new term started in January, Niemöller settled down to work, the curriculum including ecclesiastical history with special reference to the Reformation, dogma and a course of lectures on the Old and New Testaments, in addition to Latin and Greek. While he studied, his wife looked after their flat, but each helped the other as need be, his wife hearing his vocabulary and Niemöller "cleaning ship", as he called it, on Saturday mornings. All his remaining spare time he devoted to the affairs of a national students' organization, which he had joined at the beginning of term.

For some weeks Niemöller was able to pursue his studies without interruption. Then, in the middle of March, a fortnight before the university term was due to end, came the abortive Kapp *Putsch*. Kapp, a right-wing politician, together with a Prussian general by the name of von Lüttwitz, who commanded a volunteer corps of ex-Servicemen, staged an armed uprising against the coalition government. After some initial success, the *Putsch* was defeated by the opposition of the Trade Unions. Kapp escaped to Sweden, but later voluntarily returned to Germany where he died while in prison awaiting trial. Meanwhile the lecture halls at Münster University were seething with rumours. Niemöller and his fellow right-wing German Nationals believed that their hour had struck and, while the fate of the Kapp *Putsch* still hung in the balance, walked out of a lecture on Westphalian Church history to bring into being an organization that they had long been planning. This was the Academic Defence Corps, a fighting unit of right-wing students which they now proposed to organize and train in readiness to support the new Kapp government. But that government never materialized, and instead of a victory for conservatism, Kapp's attempted rebellion brought about a serious threat to the Weimar Constitution from the extreme Left: the Communists seized power in the industrial areas of Rhineland-Westphalia.

With the defeat of their political ally, Kapp, the members of the Academic Defence Corps now shelved their hostility to "The System" and waited impatiently for the government to arm them and order them to march in the cause of law and order. But the government was in no hurry to put its dubious allies into the field, and it was not until the Communists, who had also organized themselves into fighting battalions, were nearing Münster on their triumphal march from the Rhine that the Academic Defence Corps was called upon to stop them. The response was immediate. Right-wing students abandoned their studies and flocked to fight under the anti-Red banner. By 20 March university lecturers were finding themselves without an audience and, despite the protests of a minority of Socialist students, the university was closed.

Meanwhile the members of the Academic Defence Corps, now numbering 750, were drawing arms and equipment from a disused Army barracks on the fringe of the city. Divided into three battalions, of which one was commanded by Martin Niemöller, they were mostly ex-soldiers and so required little training and within ten days the Corps was ready for action.

The fratricidal campaign which then began lasted barely a month. Shortly before Easter, the Defence Corps moved off south-westwards towards the Reds who were still advancing, though more slowly now, from the direction of the Rhine. Elements of the two forces met on the line of the River Lippe, south of Münster, and a series of skirmishes developed in which both sides used artillery. At daybreak on Good Friday, the Communists sent up some aircraft, but without noticeable effect on the fighting, and on Easter Day the Academic Defence Corps together with units of the new Regular Army crossed the river and occupied a number of pit-heads and mining villages on the far bank.

Niemöller and his men were then given the task of making a house to house search for arms and also of arresting the ringleaders of the Red revolt, who were known to be in the neighbourhood. Weapons were not difficult to find, but the wanted men proved more elusive. Those few who were captured were sent to Münster under armed guard, only to be released later under a general amnesty. Having survived the Kapp *Putsch* and the Communist insurrection the coalition government were more interested in pacification than reprisals, and in an early disarming of all military forces, whether of the Right or Left. The Academic Defence Corps was accordingly allowed to continue its advance only as far as Bochum, the coalmining centre in the Ruhr, whence the entire force was transported back to Münster and ordered to disband.

During the fighting the Niemöllers' first child had been born, a girl, whom they christened Brigitte. No doubt his family responsibilities helped Niemöller to settle down to study again when the new university term began soon after the end of his military excursion, and also to refuse a tempting invitation which he received in April to join the newly formed Reichswehr, or regular army, with the rank of Captain. Two other offers, though financially more rewarding, required less resolution to refuse: the position of works manager in a large industrial concern and, in the following August, an inquiry from a Berlin firm as to whether Niemöller would undertake to deliver a ship-load of munitions to Turkey, which was then at war with Greece, in return for a very considerable payment. Financially the offer was tempting, but with the British in control of the Dardanelles there seemed small chance of the ship reaching her destination. Moreover Niemöller had already broken, painfully enough, with a sailor's life and ever since had studiously avoided even the sight of the sea. Was it worth re-opening old wounds for the sake of so short-lived and hazardous an adventure? Niemöller hesitated and meanwhile, fortunately for him, someone else got the job. Sure enough, in due course the ship was intercepted by the British Navy and it was many months before the crew could return to Germany.

Having resisted the temptation to be deflected from his studies, Niemöller now faced a new threat to their continuation. Hitherto, he had been supporting his wife and himself on his naval pension, though inflation had been steadily reducing its value. Now, at the end of February, 1922, he would have either to find some extra source of income or else leave the university. To tide them over, Niemöller tried to sell the only object of real value which he and his wife possessed—a Luther Bible printed in 1545 by Hans Lufft in Wittenberg. But the offers he received were too small to justify parting with a treasured heirloom. Soon after, his brother-in-law, who had just been appointed deputy head of a big hospital in Göttingen, came to his rescue with a substantial sum of money which sufficed to keep the family going for some months. Then, in July, 1922, a son was born, christened Hans Jochen in memory of a submariner friend.

"There was now another mouth to feed," Niemöller recalls, "and the value of money was still falling and I still had one more term to go before my first theological examination, and then a whole year before my second. The prospects were not rosy; in fact, we were up against it. . . ." At the end of July, Niemöller got a spare-time job as plate-layer on the railways. It was hard work, harder, even, than coaling ship had been in the Navy, but it kept the family alive. After seven weeks, he was transferred to the engine-sheds and, ten days later, to work in the shunting-yard at Münster Station. Meanwhile, the staff of the railway accounts office were in despair. Salary scales, rates of pension and allowances—every single charge or payment made by the State Railways was becoming obsolete almost before it could be revised. Calculations that had once been simple and rapidly made were being transformed by inflation into a nightmare. Early in October, the accountants were in need of reinforcement and Niemöller was again transferred, this time to an office stool. Until January, 1923, he struggled to preserve order amid financial chaos, emerging from the ordeal addled, exhausted and convinced that the automatic adding machine would prove an unparalleled boon to mankind.

Inflation was now at its height. On Monday a loaf of bread might cost a million marks; on Tuesday, two million. Wages throughout Germany were being doubled and redoubled by employers in a frantic effort to preserve their workmen from starvation. They were no longer paid weekly now, but daily, so that immediately he had been paid, a man could buy food for his family, knowing that by next morning his wage-packet would have become almost worthless. Each day when he went to work, Niemöller took a rucksack with him, bringing home potatoes, meat and bread when he returned at night. Despite these precautions and his hard work, his family would have gone hungry at times if his wife had not unpicked the gold lace from his old uniforms which he then sold to a jeweller for melting down. For a whole fortnight the family lived on the money realized by selling a ship's chronometer which Niemöller had kept as a souvenir of his U-boat days.

These were typical of the expedients which every German was forced to take at that time in order to stay alive, and as a direct result of the Allies' financial and reparations policy towards Germany. Until this was reversed, no amount of hard work would enable Germany to recover or the tide of inflation to be halted. Understandably, feeling against the Allies ran high and in the early summer of 1922 the German Foreign Minister, Rathenau, was assassinated by Right-wing fanatics for conducting, as they considered, too conciliatory a policy towards Britain, France and America. The German trade unions then proclaimed a general strike. Meanwhile, Hitler's National Socialist Party, founded three years previously in Munich, had been growing in strength and by January, 1923, had enough supporters to hold its first National Rally. In the same month, the occupation of the Ruhr began and for seventeen months, until July, 1924, upwards of ten thousand French troops, including Africans, were billeted in Germany's richest industrial area, bringing production to a standstill and throwing millions of Germans out of work. To these troops and to the policy which brought them to Germany, Adolf Hitler owed no small debt of gratitude.

On the same day that Frenchmen were marching into the Ruhr and Germans were retaliating with passive resistance, Niemöller submitted two theses to the Consistorial Board in Münster, comprising the written work that had been set for his first examination in theology. The subjects were: "Was Paul a true witness of Jesus Christ?" and "The Mysticism of Meister Eckart and of Bernhard of Clairveaux." He then started preparing for the oral examination which was to take place in the following April. This included a subject of which he knew precisely nothing—the history of philosophy. His brother, who was also entering the Church, was in the same predicament. For an hour each day they tramped through the countryside asking one another questions from a little book which the publishers claimed gave "all the answers". They learnt them by heart, from cover to cover, and in due course their faith was rewarded, for it was the author of the book who examined them.

After passing the oral examination, Niemöller took up his first appointment in the Church, as curate to the pastor in whose rectory he and his wife were living. His main duties consisted in taking services for children, preparing candidates for confirmation and visiting aged and sick parishioners, while the pastor devoted several hours each week to discussing the general running of a parish with him. This method of initiation seemed to Niemöller ideal and it was with great regret that, two months later, he lost his mentor, Pastor Kähler, on the latter's appointment to the Bishopric of Stettin.

Niemöller was now left in sole charge of the parish. Among his flock were refugees from Posen and West Prussia, billeted in a former prisoner-of-war camp on the outskirts of Münster, and a handful of Protestants living in the nearby town of Telgte, famous for its Catholic shrine. In both places Niemöller held services and preached, finding inspiration in the faith and sincerity of his congregations. Yet two years before, the mere thought of having to deliver a sermon had filled him with dread. Even now, sometimes, as he sat in his attic room, puffing out clouds of tobacco smoke and making notes for his Sunday sermon, he would remember that unnerving ordeal when he had preached the first sermon of his life in a chapel at Münster before the Professor of Homiletics and a score of theological students.

Niemöller had spent a whole week learning the sermon by heart and the set text was a fine one: "My soul doth magnify the Lord and my spirit hath rejoiced in God my Saviour." Yet, after a good start he had lost the sequence of thought and got hopelessly stuck, then somehow had managed to continue for a few minutes until he had dried up a second time. . . .

That night Niemöller was in despair. If only he had been preaching to friends, a real congregation, instead of to a hypercritical audience of fellow-students! He had something to say, he knew that, but the atmosphere in chapel had been too artificial and he had succumbed to examination nerves. Then suddenly Niemöller had an idea. Telephoning his father, he explained his plight and asked whether on the following Sunday he might be allowed to preach the sermon in his father's church at Elberfeld. Every member of the congregation would be known to him. He felt sure he would not let him down. His father agreed, and a few days later Niemöller preached again on the text: "My soul doth magnify the Lord. . . ." This time, as he spoke, the sublime faith of the Magnificat calmed his mind and his fears left him, never to return. "Since that fourth Sunday in Advent," writes Niemöller, "it has not been the act of preaching which has worried me, but the content of my sermons. Have I really spoken in God's Name, and in accordance with His Will?"

For Niemöller the summer of 1923 was an exacting period. Though still only a curate, he was acting as pastor of a parish and, as his salary was not enough even to feed his family, working as well in the railway accountant's office at night. In addition, there was his second theological examination to prepare for and another thesis to write on the subject: "The uses and limitations of the Psychological-Religious Method". Hard pressed, undernourished and concerned for the future of his family, Niemöller had need of all his stamina. Meanwhile there still hovered at the back of his mind the dream that had been inseparable from his first resolve to enter the Church—the dream of a country parish of his own, an orderly life for himself and his flock, contentment, and the Peace of God.

Chapter Four

THE WESTPHALIAN HOME MISSION

(1923–31)

IN the early winter of 1923 Niemöller was offered an appointment which meant postponing indefinitely all hopes of a country parish: the Church government of Münster asked him to become Manager for Westphalia of the Protestant Home Mission. This was an administrative post involving considerable responsibility and the offer was as flattering as it was unexpected. All the same, Niemöller hesitated before accepting. The "Home Mission" had been founded by the nineteenth-century Hamburg theologian, Johann Hinrich Wichern (1808-81) and in course of time had come to cover all the social welfare activities of the Evangelical Church, both voluntary and official. The post of manager would bring Niemöller into touch with members of the organization, but hardly at all, he feared, with the people for whose benefit it existed. It offered nothing remotely akin to the relationship between a pastor and his parishioners. But—a deciding factor in view of Niemöller's struggle to make both ends meet—it carried with it a salary large enough to provide him and his family with complete security. So he accepted.

By 1 December, 1923, the day on which Niemöller took up his new appointment, the worst of the inflation was over. The German Government had succeeded in stabilizing the mark by the drastic measure of currency reform. A limited period of time was allotted during which the banks would accept the existing Reichsmark in payment for the new Rentenmark, exchanging them at the rate of a billion for one. At the end of that time, the old currency would become invalid and any sums still held by private individuals would be worthless. Though private savings were thus wiped out overnight, the very severity of the measure convinced the British, French and American Governments that Germany was in earnest and for the first time since the war the German Government was thereafter able to borrow money, mostly from the U.S.A. Meanwhile the German people had set to work as never before to earn enough to keep alive. As for Niemöller, he more than most had cause to be relieved at the stabilization of the mark, for his new duties involved amongst other things the management of considerable sums of money.

The new manager started in a modest setting. One small room in the Deaconess' Institute in Münster had to serve as an office and its entire equipment consisted of a desk, two chairs, an antique typewriter, an empty filing cabinet and a female secretary considerably advanced in years. Niemöller's main task was to try to centralize the voluntary and official welfare activities of the Home Mission and link them more closely with those in the individual parishes. At the same time, he had to ensure that the Home Mission lost none of its independence in the process, and this was a particularly important consideration in Westphalia, where Friedrich von Bodelschwingh (1831-1910) had developed the Home Mission hospitals in Bethel into the world famous sanatoria for epileptics which bear his name and where, therefore, the tradition of effective independent action was particularly strong.

As a result of the war and the ensuing inflation, it was the hospitals, their equipment and staffing which became Niemöller's most urgent practical problem. Buildings were falling into disrepair, some even were derelict, while those members of the staffs who had survived the war were mostly due for retirement. In their stead, large numbers of nursing sisters and social welfare workers were needed who had received modern training and were "drawn from life", to borrow Niemöller's phrase, as distinct from those circles in pre-war society where it had been accounted the prerogative of the ladies to indulge in charitable activities without any specialist knowledge. Finally, youth hostels, homes for the aged and kindergartens—as yet existing only on paper—had somehow to be built in the larger towns and suitable staff recruited and trained to run them.

The first essential, if this programme was to be fulfilled, was to obtain the necessary money. For this purpose, Niemöller founded the Evangelical Savings Society, registering the first savings book in his own name. The scheme was an immediate success and by 1931 the total deposits had reached the formidable figure of 15 million marks. Still flourishing, the society celebrated its twenty-fifth anniversary in 1953 and continues to function today. Amongst the building construction financed by this means is a large sanatorium, in Niemöller's birthplace of Lippstadt, for the treatment of tuberculosis of the bone. As regards the staffing problem, Niemöller set up a special training school for women welfare workers, teaching there himself for a few hours each week, while in order to obtain the large number of girls required for hospital work, he supported measures designed to make the career of nursing sister more attractive.

In addition to his work in the Home Mission, on which Niemöller submitted progress reports at regular intervals to the Provincial Synod, he was appointed in this period to a vacancy on the Consistory Board. As assistant to the General Superintendent, Niemöller worked in a number of administrative capacities and found his duties extraordinarily diverse and interesting. Finally, in May, 1924, he passed his second theological examination for which he had been preparing when appointed to the Home Mission, and on 29 June in that year he was ordained in the Church of the Redeemer in Münster, preaching the sermon on a text from the Epistle to the Philippians: "Not as though I had already attained, either were already perfect. . . ."

On his way home after his second theological examination, Niemöller had a conversation which was to give him food for thought for many months to come. Walking with the Professor in Ordinary of Systematic Theology at Münster University, Professor Wehrüng, Niemöller took the opportunity of asking his advice in a matter which had been on his mind for some time. Due perhaps to the insight which his work on the Board of Consistory gave him into the friction which often arose between the administrators of the Church and the individual parishes, Niemöller was then particularly concerned with this question: what is the ideal relationship between the Church and the parishes? Or, in other words: "what is the essential meaning of the expression, 'the Church'?"

It is typical of the attitude which many orthodox theologians of that time adopted to this question, that the Professor—who, incidentally, was a disciple of Albert Schweitzer's—merely gave an embarrassed smile and said: "Why do you worry about the Church? Is it so important?"

In later years Niemöller looked back on this conversation with the comment: "I think it was then that I acquired what I might call my Congregationalist leaning."* Meanwhile, as time passed he came to see the whole problem of the relationship between the central authority and the men "in the field" against the background of the strongly independent and thriving Westphalian parishes. It is understandable, therefore, that even at that time the question exercised him as to whether the functions and title of a bishop properly belonged to the Evangelical Church. Since the disappearance of the traditional German State Church, the question had become a highly topical one and was under passionate discussion everywhere, even in the Synods of the Prussian Church. There were some provincial Churches which seemed unable to dispense with the title of Bishop; others, where it was firmly and emphatically rejected. The controversy raged with particular fervour in the two western Church provinces of the Rhineland and Westphalia, until the opinion finally prevailed that, though the title of Bishop—adopted by

---

* Congregationalism is defined as a system of ecclesiastical polity that leaves legislative, disciplinary and judicial functions to the individual Church. *Translator.*

some few Lutheran Churches—might be harmless enough in itself, it could all too easily lead to the holder assuming the functions of a Bishop which, as was generally agreed, were entirely opposed to Evangelical tradition, and it was decided that the title itself should not be introduced in those two provinces.

Though at that time Niemöller himself could not come to a clear decision on this question, experience taught him at any rate one valuable lesson, namely, that in the life of the Church the centre of gravity must lie with the parishes. If the parishes were "dead", then no administrative action by a bishop, however enlightened, could bring them to life again. A freshly confirmed youth who had the sanction of Holy Writ possessed more authority than the most powerful of bishops when the latter's relation to Holy Writ had become somewhat equivocal. That was Niemöller's firm conviction, and it was to remain so even when, years later, he himself stood at the head of a great Provincial Church after emphatically declining the title of Bishop.

From this attitude to a bishop's functions it was only a small step to the opinion of "Confessions" within the Evangelical Church which Niemöller gradually formed during those years. Certainly—"*we* stand on the shoulders of our forefathers", and he believed that, and believing it, accepted Confessional differences and even, when necessary, their right to be respected, but nevertheless he was equally convinced that the Confessions had only relative value, represented as it were a "provisional attitude" and no more than that, and hence lost their value and their *raison d'être* as soon as absolute rights were claimed for them. In later years, particularly during the restoration of the German Churches after 1945, this attitude was not a popular one and Niemöller's insistence in giving it public expression aroused considerable strife. But having been born in a Lutheran parish within the "Union",* Niemöller spoke from personal

* The Evangelical Union of 1817 originated in the Duchy of Nassau and was later introduced into the Kingdom of Prussia and a number of other German Provinces. From it arose the United Lutheran-Reformed Churches. Among these is the Church of Hessen-Nassau, of which Martin Niemöller is President.

experience and refused to abandon his opinions, even though, for the second time in his life, they were to make him the object of violent criticism on the part of many of his fellow-churchmen.

Profitable and instructive as they were, these years entailed long periods of separation from his family. Much of the time was spent in travelling to all parts of Westphalia, and occasionally farther afield, in the small motor car which had been allocated to him for his official duties. In course of time, these journeys became increasingly necessary and in the years 1927 to 1930, Niemöller spent an average of 200 days annually on the road. His travels were not lacking, of course, in incident, though mostly of an amusing nature. In the Westphalian town of Hamm, however, whose marshalling yards were so frequently the target of Allied air raids during the Second World War, Niemöller was nearly involved in a fatal accident. One Saturday afternoon in 1929, Niemöller was on his way to the railway station to meet a friend. Being late, he was getting all the speed he could out of the little car when a lorry came suddenly across his front. He braked hard—the car skidded, turned over, and he was trapped underneath. The accident had occurred in front of an inn where a wedding reception was being held. Bride, bridegroom and guests rushed out and by a combined effort succeeded in righting Niemöller's car. Apart from a bad fright he received no ill effects, while the car was undamaged except for the near-side direction indicator. But the main thing was that he reached the station in time to meet the train!

Even when Niemöller was at home, work still claimed most of his time. His flat and office were now in a large, two-storeyed house which he had commissioned to his own design soon after his appointment to the Home Mission. A gift of 4000 dollars had helped considerably in a total cost of 35,000 marks. Attached to the house was a garden where his children could play. There were now six: Brigitte, Jochen, Heinz Hermann (1924), Jan (1925), Hertha (1927) and Jutta (1928). On the few evenings which Niemöller could spend with his family and friends they would read the mad adventures of Baron von Romberg, the Westphalian "national hero", or else the General Superintendent, Zöllner, would come and play duets with Niemöller on the piano and harmonium. Sometimes, when old U-boat friends* were present, they would spend the evening reminiscing about their war experiences. On Sundays, sometimes, Niemöller would take a walk with the children or go rowing on the river.

It was not until 1927, when his eldest daughter, Brigitte, started to attend school in Münster, that Niemöller came to realize the full plight of the Evangelical schools in that predominantly Catholic city. He then discovered that all too little had been done to support them financially. Their need led him to his first incursion into politics. He founded an Evangelical group on the Münster City Council comprising seven members without party-political allegiance. Niemöller was leader of the group for two years and succeeded in that time in making common cause with the Roman Catholics on many matters of mutual concern, thus presenting with them a united front to the Prussian State, which at that time was governed by a Socialist Clerical Coalition. When Niemöller ultimately left Münster the Catholic mayor of the city, Doctor Sperling, paid tribute to his work in a cordial farewell speech and presented him with a bronze letter-weight and a decorated plate showing the coat-of-arms of the city in the traditional colours of red, white and gold with the motto: *Ehr is Dwang nog*, meaning "Honour is Discipline enough".

Yet even in those days Niemöller had no intention of taking up politics. "I am no politician"—more than once he has said this when friends or opponents try to divert him into the sphere of party politics. It is not surprising therefore that he has never in his life been a member of a party. His work on the Münster City Council was only an episode. The brief entry, "much

---

* Among these was Wilhelm Canaris, later the Admiral and head of Hitler's Intelligence Service. He and Niemöller had met during the First World War when each had been commanding a U-boat in the Mediterranean. Canaris was hanged by Hitler's S.S. on 9 April, 1945.

work", which repeatedly appears in his diaries of that period, refers almost invariably to his work as a churchman, not as a local government politician, and Church work was indeed varied and interesting enough.

Niemöller's first active encounter with the wireless also belongs in these years. His claustrophobia and stage fright were considerable to start with, almost as great as when he had preached his first sermon to a congregation of professors and students of theology and got stuck in the middle. Yet when he first stood before the microphone, or "whisper-disc" as it was called, the realization that he was among friends immediately banished his fear. From then on it never returned. A chance encounter on the day following his first broadcast helped to achieve that result. An old gardener who knew him by sight came up to Niemöller in the street and congratulated him on his "fine talk on the wireless". The tribute meant more to Niemöller than the approval of his colleagues, particularly as the old man was a Roman Catholic.

Though Niemöller learnt to know his own capabilities in these years, particularly as an administrator and organizer, and he gained valuable experience in public affairs, he had never intended to spend the rest of his life as a Church manager, and as time passed he longed increasingly to do the work which had been the background to his life from the day he was born—that of pastor of a parish. At last, despite the financial security which his appointments on the Consistory Board and in the Home Mission afforded, he decided to relinquish them both. He was entitled to give six months' notice at any time and he accordingly did so, in face of his father's vigorous protests, on 1 January, 1931.

During the six months' interval before his resignation became effective, he received three offers of a parish. The first, which he declined, was in the industrial centre of Essen. Soon after, he was invited to become pastor of a parish in Bielefeld. Niemöller was on the point of accepting when he discovered that the parish council had been unanimous in selecting him with the exception of one member, the man with whom Niemöller would have to work in close accord—the other curate of Bielefeld. Very reluctantly, Niemöller then felt he ought to refuse. Months passed during which Niemöller celebrated his thirty-ninth birthday, and then in the late spring he received an unexpected invitation to fill a vacancy as third and junior pastor in the Berlin suburb of Dahlem, one of the wealthiest and most sought-after parishes in Prussia. Niemöller was disposed to accept. He had liked what he had seen of Berlin on his periodic visits and the cosmopolitan atmosphere of the capital with its world-wide connexions had appealed to him. But first, he went to Dahlem to make the acquaintance of the two pastors who would become his colleagues. Finding that they all got on well together, he accepted the invitation and arranged to start work in the parish on 1 July, 1931, the day on which his appointment in Westphalia ended.

It was in the early hours of the morning when Martin Niemöller got home from Berlin and the children were all in bed. At the first sound of their father's footfall, they were sitting bolt upright, waiting breathlessly for the news. As soon as they heard it, there was a deluge of questions: "How big will our house be?" "Shall we go sailing on the Wannsee?" "Are there any trees in Berlin?" and "Do they have trams as in Münster?"

Before they moved, Niemöller and his wife went on holiday, leaving the children with his parents. Thus they both got a rest —he, from his official duties, and Frau Niemöller from managing her large family. Borrowing the car he had used on his official journeys for the Home Mission, Niemöller took his wife on a tour of all the loveliest and most romantic places in western Germany, starting with the Rhine castles and the Taunus Mountains, then continuing on to Heidelberg, where they stood on the terrace of the castle and gazed at the fabulous view down the valley of the Neckar, thence through Heilbronn to Stuttgart. From Stuttgart, they visited the old Franconian towns of

Nördlingen, Dinkelsbühl, Rothenburg, Nürnberg and Miltenberg, the tour finally ending in Elberfeld. In the prime of life, with solid achievement behind him and the sure fulfilment of his dream gilding the future, Niemöller spent those weeks in a mood of timeless happiness. Even today, after more than twenty-five years, he can remember every detail of the sights, the people they met, and their times together on that holiday which he and his wife spent as young people before persecution laid its blight upon them.

Soon after, they and their family were on their way by train to Berlin. Throughout the journey, the girls each clutched a jar of tropical fish from the aquarium they had kept at home. Sometimes a shaft of sunlight would strike golden glints from their scales.

In 1931 Dahlem, a suburb to the southwest of Berlin, was accounted one of the richest parishes in Germany. Here at St. Anne's Church, in July of that year, Niemöller became junior pastor

Chapter Five

PASTOR *versus* STATE

(1931–6)

THE suburb of Dahlem lies to the south-west of Berlin adjoining the area known as the Grunewald. With its lakes,
bathing beaches and wooded hills, the Grunewald is the Berliner's favourite week-end resort, while Dahlem itself has developed rapidly during the last fifty years into a select residential
colony dotted with the villas of the well-to-do. The parish had
been created in 1918 and was accounted one of the wealthiest in
Germany. Bankers, industrialists, politicians, people from the
film and theatre world, comprised the flock for whose spiritual
welfare Niemöller was to share responsibility. "You'll find it
difficult to come to grips with them," a friend warned him. "It's
like trying to bite on cotton-wool."

But, free at last to devote himself to the twin tasks which were
the essence of his calling—preaching and the cure of souls—
Niemöller was not to be discouraged. Inducted into his new
office in the parish church of Saint Anne in July, 1931, less than
six months later he was appointed head pastor on the death of
his senior colleague. He then moved into the rectory, a red brick
building overgrown with creeper and set in a large garden which
included a lawn surrounded with silver firs and fruit-trees. A
small doorway led directly from the garden to the adjoining
churchyard. The ancient little church, built of untrimmed
granite blocks, had become too small for the growing parish,
and before the end of Niemöller's first year in Dahlem a large
new building had been completed and consecrated.

Though Niemöller no longer panicked at the thought of preaching, he still found it a difficult task as, indeed, it ought to be when conscientiously performed. From the start he considered the weekly sermon to be one of his most important duties. Unlike the majority of successful preachers, he abhorred theatrical effects. The pathos, the rhetoric, the fine frenzies to which so many parsons give free rein in the pulpit found no place in Niemöller's sermons. He never preached extempore, but thought out and then wrote out what he had to say in full, from the first word to the last. He kept strictly to the prescribed passages of the Bible, interpreting them with a simple, orthodox piety which allowed of no subjective deviations. Thus, in later years when his fame as a preacher had become established, some who came to hear him went away disappointed. Accustomed to the gusty emotionalism of political speakers, they found Niemöller's style altogether too astringent.

Second in importance to preaching, Niemöller considered, was the preparation of candidates for confirmation. Each week he held ten or more classes for some hundreds of children in the Dahlem parish hall.

Sometimes Church business would call him away from the parish for a few days; then he would travel all night rather than have to cancel one of these classes. For his adult parishioners he instituted fortnightly "Catechism Classes"; later, under the name of "Open Evenings", these were to play an important part in the so-called Battle of the Protestant Churches. Finally, visiting took up a great deal of Niemöller's time. Here he took a leaf out of his father's book, setting himself a definite number of parishioners to call on each day, so that he could be sure of having spoken to each of them personally by the end of the year. In these and other tasks, the years 1931 and 1932 quickly passed. Niemöller has called them the happiest of his life. Certainly they were the calmest and perhaps the most satisfying, for never— before or since—has he been able to devote all his energies to work in a parish of his own. Suggestions for different employment, which at one time he might have found tempting, were now turned down without hesitation. The first came from Admiral Raeder, then Chief of Naval Staff in Berlin, who offered him the post of garrison chaplain in Kiel. Six months later he was invited to join the training ship *Emden* as padre and sail in her on a world cruise.

Meanwhile, political events in Germany were disturbing. In February, 1932, the number of unemployed rose to over six million. In July, the National Socialist Party polled twice the number of votes it had received in the previous elections and its representation in the Reichstag was increased to 230. In November, the Church elections brought Niemöller into contact for the first time with the "German Christians", a movement openly prepared to subordinate Christianity to National Socialism and brought into being only five months previously. Hitherto, the German Christians had achieved little success, and no one had taken them very seriously. But from now on, the movement became one of Hitler's chief weapons in the Battle of the Protestant Churches, and much to his disgust, Niemöller had a number of its members sitting on his own parish council.

The threat which Hitler and his German Christians represented to the teaching of Christ's Gospel in Germany was slow to develop. Article 24 of the Nazi Party Programme had expressed the intention to foster "positive Christianity", a reassuringly respectable phrase which the German Christians repeated in declaring their aim to be the renewal of the Church "on the basis of positive Christianity and in the spirit of Martin Luther". Even after he became Reich Chancellor in January, 1933, Hitler himself continued to speak soft words to the German Churches. "I look on the two main Christian denominations," he declared, "as the bed-rock of State and family life," and went on to say that the relationship between the Churches and the State would remain unchanged, and that the rights of the Churches would be upheld in their entirety. Many churchmen took these statements at their face value and allowed themselves to be deluded into thinking that some sort of co-operation would, after all, be possible between the author of *Mein Kampf* and the Churches. Some even were to quote them as justification for their own failure to take a more resolute stand against National Socialism. Finally, a few churchmen surrendered to the optimistic dream of enlisting Hitler's aid in bringing about the fusion of the twenty-eight different Protestant Churches into a single German Evangelical Church.

Not all Protestant churchmen were so weak or foolish, and more than one voice was raised in warning, the most forthright being perhaps that of the Church President and later Bishop of Württemberg, Doctor Wurm. Dr. Wurm reminded the over-zealous that to talk of reorganizing the Evangelical Church was to lower it to the status of a mutual aid society, but in the event, the warnings of Wurm and others came too late. The German Christians were becoming continually more extravagant and aggressive in their demands and under the cry of *Gleichschaltung*, or "co-ordination", they were already aiming at nothing less than the complete subordination of the Churches to the State.

In April, 1933, a committee of three men, representing the German Protestant Churches, started to draw up proposals for the "reorganization" allegedly so long overdue. Beginning their labours with a statement expressing "a grateful 'yes' " to the opportunity held out to them by the *Führer* and thanking God who "has brought us to this turning point in our history", they failed nevertheless to convince Hitler of their reliability and he appointed a personal representative to supervise their work. This plenipotentiary of the Reich Chancellor, as he was called, was a fifty-year-old ex-Army chaplain by the name of Ludwig Müller. "Müller of Königsberg" had recently been appointed head of the German Christians. Within a month the committee produced a report recommending the creation of a unified German Evangelical Church headed by a Reich Bishop of the Lutheran creed. No doubt Müller had earmarked this post for

Superintendent Richter, Pastor von Bodelschwingh and Superintendent-General Karow at the installation of von Bodelschwingh as Reich Bishop in Berlin, 1933. Pastor Niemöller stands immediately behind von Bodelschwingh and half-right behind him is standing Pastor Stratenwerth himself, but at the Church elections on 27 May the delegates passed over him in favour of the Westphalian pastor, Friedrich von Bodelschwingh, who accordingly became the first Reich Bishop. Among the reasons for Müller's defeat was no doubt the fact that the German Christians had recently amended the Church marriage service to conform with the Nazi racial laws. This evidence of the German Christians' increasing subservience to Hitler, together, perhaps, with the first rumours of Nazi concentration camps, sufficed to ensure Müller's defeat.

The new Reich Bishop was the grandson of a Prussian Minister of the Interior. Bodelschwingh was also head of the Evangelical hospitals of the Home Mission in Bethel, which had been named Bodelschwingh Institutions after his father who had founded them. Much as he disliked the authoritarian sound of the title "Reich Bishop", Bodelschwingh accepted the post and named two Westphalian colleagues to assist him: Martin Niemöller and Gerhard Stratenwerth.

A principal task of the triumvirate was to consider in detail the constitution of the newly formed German Evangelical Church. Like Bodelschwingh, Niemöller assumed that Hitler would honour his self-declared intention not to interfere with internal Church affairs and hence would accept whatever decisions they reached. That hope was quickly dispelled. Not merely the German Christians, but the government itself attempted to interfere with the framing of the constitution, and when that proved impossible, insisted that it should be submitted to them for approval. Bodelschwingh held out for as long as he could, but when, on 24 June, the government appointed a State official to supervise the Prussian Church on the pretext that internal dissensions threatened to bring about its collapse, he resigned. His tenure of office as Reich Bishop had lasted exactly four weeks.

Belonging to a "United" Church, Bodelschwingh had been scrupulous in consulting the interests of all Protestant Creeds when acting as Reich Bishop. As time passed and churchmen realized that Hitler's object was not to strengthen the Churches, but to subordinate them, in common with all other German institutions, to his supreme control, the loss of Bodelschwingh's non-partisan outlook became increasingly felt.

Niemöller, meanwhile, had returned to his parish duties in Dahlem. Having had personal experience of Hitler's methods of attaining his ends in Church affairs, it came as no surprise to him when a revised constitution for the German Evangelical Church was drafted in accordance with the government's wishes, and put into effect in the short space of twenty-one days, to be followed immediately by the *Führer's* decree for the holding of new Church elections. Hitler's object was, of course, to stage a resounding victory for the German Christians and when they began their electoral campaign, they were given free use of the Nazi propaganda machine. "The National Socialist State," they declared in a pamphlet, "will not tolerate institutions within its boundaries which persist in maintaining an attitude of independence or neutrality." When the aged President Hindenburg expressed concern as a Protestant at the policy and methods of the German Christians, Hitler hastened to reassure him personally. On the eve of poll he intervened again in a radio speech in which he recommended the German Christians and the would-be Reich Bishop, Ludwig Müller, to his listeners and delivered an undisguised threat to their opponents.

The result of the elections was thus a foregone conclusion. Vilified as "politically unreliable", even as "enemies of the State", the Protestant opposition succumbed almost everywhere to the German Christians. In some areas, where the cause of the opposition seemed particularly hopeless, the ecclesiastical office-holders resigned even before the election results were announced. In Dahlem and a few other parishes, on the other hand, the German Christians were in the minority. Nevertheless, their overall victory enabled them henceforth to impose their authority on the other Churches and pursue their policy of *Gleichschaltung* at will.

The German Christians now began to ape the arrogant and aggressive methods of their political masters. A meeting of the General Synod for Prussia, where they held a two-thirds majority, broke up in disorder and seventy-one delegates walked out, headed by Dr. Koch, the President of the Westphalian Church. Niemöller had declined to attend the Divine Service which opened this "Brown Synod" and to make his protest more apparent, had arrived for the meeting dressed in a pale grey suit instead of in black. Three weeks later he addressed a circular letter to all German pastors inviting them to join a "Pastors' Emergency Union" and give the written undertaking "to abide only by the Holy Scriptures and the tenets of the Reformation and conscientiously to care for those brethren who in so doing are caused to suffer unjustly". The response exceeded all expectations. By the end of September, two thousand of the fifteen thousand pastors in the whole of Germany had joined the Union. Four months later the number had risen to seven thousand. Meanwhile, on behalf of the members Niemöller addressed a declaration to the Wittenberg National Synod, distributing copies to the delegates before the start of the session and nailing further copies to the trees in front of the church, not far from the place where Luther had nailed his famous theses four hundred years before. The declaration stated: "We will not cease to work for the development of the German Evangelical Church in faithful obedience to our ordination vows."

Thus overnight almost, an unknown pastor became the mouthpiece of the German Churches' opposition to Hitler. That opposition was not, of course, political in the sense of a movement to overthrow the Nazi regime, and never was. It was confined to opposing Nazi-inspired attempts to adapt the Christian doctrine to fit in with Nazi ideology. The immediate concern was to prevent the German Christians from introducing the Nazi leadership principle and the infamous racial laws into the Protestant Church. The first directive which Niemöller issued to the members of the Emergency Union called on them to boycott a Nazi-inspired questionnaire, which had been circulated to all clergy, on the subject of their personal ancestry. Niemöller fully realized that in so doing, he was indirectly preaching disobedience of the civil power, in other words, sedition, but if someone objected: "Render under Caesar . . . ," he was ready with his answer: the distinction between an Aryan and a non-Aryan was meaningless to a Christian, for "here is neither Jew, nor Greek, but all are one in Jesus Christ".

The German Protestants were not alone in their rejection of the Nazi racial laws. At a meeting in Sofia, the World Alliance for Co-operation between the Churches called these laws "a denial of our Lord, Jesus Christ" and protested against the intention to apply them within the German Churches, pointing out the suffering which their enforcement would entail for non-Aryan clergy. In Britain, the Bishop of Chichester addressed an open letter to the Reich Bishop on behalf of the Ecumenical Council, taking him severely to task for his authoritarian methods and stating: "The suppression and silencing of men whose views conflict with the opinions of the group at present in power is a cause of great concern to all Christians who believe in upholding freedom to preach God's Word."

Meanwhile, nine days after he had instructed the members of the Emergency Union to disregard the racial questionnaire, Niemöller was suspended from office by the Reich Bishop, Ludwig Müller. Within twenty-four hours he secured his reinstatement. Two days later he was again suspended. Finally, in February, 1934, the Bishop of Prussia placed him in permanent retirement. But while the ecclesiastical authorities vacillated, Niemöller's parishioners stood by him. By 24 votes to 15, the Dahlem Parish Council approved a declaration stigmatizing the Bishop's action as un-Christian and unconstitutional. Thereupon the Bishop retaliated by fulminating against "this open revolt against the leaders of the Church"—and in the midst of this verbal battle Niemöller continued to preach, hold services and visit his parishioners exactly as before.

Then in the last few weeks of 1933, the German Christians found themselves in serious trouble. At a great rally of their adherents held in the Berlin Sportpalast on 13 November, a certain Dr. Krause described the books of the Old Testament as "tales of whore-mongers and cattle-thieves". Another speaker declared that "the exaggerated display of the crucified Jesus is intolerable in a German church". These and similar statements were heard without protest by an audience of 20,000, among them high-ranking functionaries who owed their positions to Ludwig Müller. Their silence made the scandal if anything greater, and Niemöller for one was not prepared to bury the whole incident on the strength of official reassurances that the speakers concerned had merely been expressing their private opinions. Immediately after the rally, he protested to the Reich Bishop on behalf of the Emergency Union, calling on him to dismiss from office all bishops, pastors and church officials who had failed to protest against these blasphemous utterances. On the following Sunday, the members of the Union read a statement from their pulpits to the effect that any repetition of such heathen excesses would constitute a direct attack upon the Christian Faith.

For a while Niemöller's protests seemed unavailing. Then a split began to develop in the ranks of the German Christians and rather than see the Reich Bishop and his followers discredited, Hitler summoned the leaders of the Protestant Churches to a conference, among them, Martin Niemöller as founder of the Pastors' Emergency Union.

On the morning of the day appointed for the conference—it was 25 January, 1934—Niemöller took a taxi to the Christian Hostel in the Wilhelmstrasse where the Evangelical opponents of the German Christians had agreed to meet for prior discussion. In the hall Niemöller noticed one or two shadowy figures and concluded from their air of obtrusive self-effacement that they were eavesdroppers from the nearby Gestapo headquarters. Most of his colleagues, he discovered, held high hopes of the conference and were expecting, amongst other concessions, that Hitler would dismiss the Reich Bishop from office and eliminate the so-called "Aryan" paragraph from the new Church Constitution.

It was only a few steps to the old Reich Chancellery and the clergy went on foot, past the S.S. in their black uniforms and into a vestibule where they were told to wait. Amongst the officials moving purposefully to and fro Goering was conspicuous, in a civilian suit instead of his usual gorgeous uniform, carrying a scarlet brief-case under his arm. The clergy were ushered into Hitler's study where they found him seated at his desk, behind him, motionless as an idol, the Reich Bishop, Ludwig Müller. One by one, Frick, the Minister of the Interior, introduced the visitors and Hitler went forward to greet them. He had resumed his seat and was about to open the discussion, when Goering burst into the room, clicked his heels, gave a Nazi salute and said excitedly:

"*Herr Reichskanzler!* An hour ago Pastor Niemöller held a conversation closely connected with the subject of this conference. I ask leave to read out to you what he said."

Hitler nodded assent. It was impossible to tell from his expression whether this interlude had been planned or not, and in any case, Niemöller was at a loss at first to place the conversation that Goering recited. Then he remembered. Of course! The telephone call of that morning! He had been standing by his desk with hat and coat, ready to set out for the Wilhelmstrasse. He had given his woman secretary some last instructions for the day's work and was on the point of leaving when the phone rang. A friend of his, a Berlin theologian, wanted his views on the prospects of the conference. Niemöller quickly related what had been done to prepare the ground and said he understood that Frick desired a peaceful outcome, because of the precarious position of the Reich Bishop. Frick had apparently called on President Hindenburg, said Niemöller, to canvass his support. . . . At that point, Niemöller's secretary had called into the mouthpiece: "... and to make him give Hitler extreme unction! You must let Pastor Niemöller go now, or he will be late for the conference!"

It was the brusque but innocent remark about extreme unction which Goering now seized on. "*Mein Führer!*" he declaimed. "These people are trying to drive a wedge between yourself and the Reich President!" This touched Hitler on a sensitive spot, as Goering knew it would, and immediately he flushed with anger and started loading his guests with reproaches, treating them more like an unruly mob of children than responsible leaders of the Church. They misunderstood him, said Hitler, and misinterpreted his intentions. Peace, that was all he wanted—peace between Church and State! Yet they obstructed him, sabotaged his efforts to achieve it!

During this outburst Niemöller had come forward so as to be ready to speak as soon as he got a chance. He now tried to explain the incident, telling Hitler that the telephone conversation had been a private one and the expressions used should not be given undue weight. The remark about extreme unction had been said in haste with the sole object of putting an end to the conversation. It was perfectly innocent. Finally, said Niemöller, his own work had no other object than the welfare of the Church, the State and the German people.

Hitler had been listening in silence. Now he said brusquely: "You confine yourself to the Church. I'll take care of the German people!" Niemöller refrained from replying and Hitler seemed about to change the subject when Goering tried again. "*Herr Reichskanzler!* May I draw your attention to the fact that Pastor Niemöller is head of the Pastors' Emergency Union, which receives financial support from abroad!" There was silence, while Goering waited for his bombshell to explode. But Hitler had apparently lost interest and he passed on to the business of the conference. When it was over, Hitler once more shook hands with the clergy. When it came to his turn, Niemöller realized that this was a chance for plain speaking which might never return. Carefully choosing his words, he said:

"*Herr Reichskanzler*, you said just now: 'I will take care of the German people'. But we too, as Christians and churchmen, have a responsibility towards the German people. That responsibility was entrusted to us by God, and neither you nor anyone in this world has the power to take it from us."

For a moment Hitler stared. Then as he realized the implications of Niemöller's warning, he turned his back on him without another word.

On his way out, Niemöller saw Goering planted on a window-seat in the vestibule. Since when, he asked, had it been customary in Germany to listen-in to people's private telephone conversations? Goering made no reply. Then Niemöller said: "And what led you to make the charge that the Emergency Union receives financial support from abroad?"

"I have proof. I will send it to you," was all that Goering could find to say.

That same evening, eight Gestapo men ransacked Niemöller's rectory for incriminating material. Early one morning a few days later, a home-made bomb exploded in the hall. Though the damage was slight and no one was hurt, the police were on the scene in a matter of minutes. Yet no one had called them. They established that the perpetrator had broken in through a window, but, as Niemöller expected, he was never brought to justice.

Though alarming enough, these tokens of official displeasure were easier to bear than the reaction of some of Niemöller's colleagues to the warning he had issued to Hitler. Returning to the Christian Hostel after the abortive conference, he found himself the object of almost universal reproach. Those whose hopes of the conference had been highest were now the first to blame Niemöller for its failure. His strong words to the *Führer*, they said, had been ill-judged and ill-timed. Instead of being dismissed from office, Ludwig Müller had been strengthened in his position as Reich Bishop. One of the clergy present sought to ostracize Niemöller altogether, saying: "I see Pastor Niemöller is among us. I am not aware that we have anything further to discuss with him." Without a word, Niemöller got up and left the building.

Though there were some notable exceptions to the general safety-first attitude of the Protestant clergy, among them, Dr. Koch, the President of the Westphalian Church, their influence alone could not halt the landslide which followed. It soon became apparent that the position of the Reich Bishop had indeed been strengthened, not however because of Niemöller's courageous words to Hitler, but through the failure of so many of his former colleagues to endorse them. The first to defect from the Protestant opposition were the three provincial Bishops of Bavaria, Württemberg and Hanover, who were rash enough to give a public undertaking (later withdrawn) to obey all orders emanating from the Reich Bishop and to do all in their power to reinforce his authority. Two days after this abject capitulation, two thousand members resigned from Niemöller's Pastors' Emergency Union.

Nevertheless, many of those same men who were now deserting the opposition were to side with it again on decisive occasions in succeeding years. Their change of front was typical of many of the protagonists in the Battle of the Churches and illustrates the near impossibility of assessing, in retrospect, the contribution of Protestants, both as groups and as individuals, during the Hitler period, towards the maintenance of the Christian Faith. For the fact is that there were not always clear-cut "fronts" in the religious battles of the '30's. The German Christians and their opponents seldom comprised a solid phalanx. The issue was not a static one. There was no nailing of colours to the mast. It was a matter, rather, for those who desired to see Germany remain a Christian country to decide, each man for himself, in the light of day-to-day events just how far Hitler, his supporters, and not least the Party ideologists intended to go in elevating temporal laws above spiritual laws, the service of the community above the rights and interests of the individual and the essentially pagan philosophy of National Socialism above the teachings of Christ, and having decided that, to attempt to curb, resist or re-direct the elemental forces released by Hitler's assumption of absolute and, for the time at any rate, unchallengeable powers in a way that was both legal and effective. In these circumstances it is not surprising that practically no two churchmen held identical views on the course which it was proper for them to adopt. Moreover the protagonists in the Battle of the Churches were ordinary men liable to the ordinary human frailties. Personal ambition, timidity, indecision and opportunism were just as much in evidence as courage, consistency and Christian zeal, while amongst the Evangelical opposition, the separate interests and attitudes arising from the age-old division of German Protestantism into the Reformed, the Lutheran and the United Churches generated increasing bitterness and rivalry as the struggle progressed. In view of all these factors, it is perhaps more accurate to look on the religious battle as a series of skirmishes fought over a wide field by different bodies of men at certain intervals of time.

Meanwhile, Hitler's reaction to his warning had convinced Niemöller that the slogan "Against the German Christians, yet with Hitler" was in need of revision. Admittedly, only a few months before he and other pastors had sent Hitler a telegram congratulating him on Germany's withdrawal from the League of Nations and thanking him for his "manly act and clear statement in defence of Germany's honour". The telegram had ended with an expression of "loyal and prayerful support". But times had changed. Henceforth, Hitler and the German Christians were, for all practical purposes, synonymous. Moreover the National Socialist creed was becoming increasingly anti-Christian and anti-clerical, thanks, largely, to the efforts of the Party's ideologist, Alfred Rosenberg. An old friend of Hitler's and a participant in the abortive Munich *Putsch* in 1923, Rosenberg had been entrusted with the entire ideological and spiritual training of the Nazi Party exactly twenty-four hours before the leaders of the Protestant Churches were due to meet Hitler at the Reich Chancellery. Rosenberg's aim was the creation of a German Church in which there would be no place for the teaching of Christ. The eternal truth was not to be found in the Gospels, he proclaimed, but in the Germanic ideals of character, and education in Germany must in future be based on the "fact" that the Germanic character, not Christianity, was the source of all virtue. As for the Bible, in Rosenberg's view it was now superseded by his own book, *The Myth of the Twentieth Century*. In it he set forth the doctrine that the German people and they alone were the godhead which all Germans should worship.

In 1934 and 1935, the Protestant clergy often seemed on the point of drawing the correct conclusions from this situation, differ though they might on the question of how best to combat the new paganism and the possibility or otherwise of coming to terms with it. For now, with the creation of the "Confessing Church" out of Niemöller's Pastors' Emergency Union, a rallying ground was created for Protestants of all denominations who wished to present a united front against Hitler, and soon 800,000 Evangelical Christians in the Rhineland and Westphalia alone possessed the membership card of the new organization.

The most fateful of the meetings held under its auspices took place in May, 1934, at Barmen in the Rhineland, at which Protestants combined to issue a statement fundamentally rejecting the Nazi contention that God had revealed Himself in recent German history and in the person of Adolf Hitler. The key sentence in this statement, which was drafted by the Swiss theologian, Karl Barth, read as follows:

"Jesus Christ as He is testified to us in Holy Scripture is the one Word of God which we have to hear, trust and obey in life and in death. We reject the false doctrine that the Church might and must acknowledge as sources of its proclamation except and beside this one Word of God still other events, powers, forms and truths as God's revelation."

In the autumn of the same year, the second Synod of the Confessing Church met in Dahlem and spoke a yet clearer language. The Council of Brethren of the German Evangelical Church, which had grown out of the managing committee of the Emergency Union, once again warned the parish clergy not to obey the instructions of the Reich Bishop and his functionaries, since, in the words of Niemöller's own choosing: "to obey these despots of the Church is to disobey God". At the conclusion of the Synod, the leaders of the Confessing Church branded the German Christians with the "Protestant Anathema", pronouncing a phrase which had not been heard in Germany for centuries: "Through them Satan pursues his ends."

In making these declarations, the Confessing Church was, in effect, claiming to be the only true Evangelical Church in Germany, with authority derived neither from the State nor from any other ecclesiastical body, but directly from the Word of God. From now on until his arrest in the summer of 1937, Niemöller stubbornly resisted all attempts wherever they arose to dispute that claim or rob it of its finality by offers of mediation. Such dangers were real enough, for despite the apparent solidarity which prevailed at Barmen and Dahlem, there were certain groups within the Protestant Church which were averse to destroying the last possibility of compromise with the German Christians, notably, the Lutheran Churches who were prepared to sacrifice much for the sake of achieving their long cherished aim of a united Lutheran Church. Thus even the first Reich Bishop, von Bodelschwingh, who had never previously temporized with the German Christians, could not now bring himself to make a clean break, but sought to preserve some link with them and the so-called neutrals, though to many "confessing" churchmen the latter were, if anything, the more objectionable of the two. Finally, a number of those who were favourably inclined to the Confessing Church nevertheless agreed with the well-known writer, Jochen Klepper, when he reproached them with being too uncompromising. "They are too busy raising

Pastor Niemöller, a photograph taken in 1935 at
Dahlem

barriers and their militant professions of faith drown the message of love."

While others weakened in their resistance to the German Christians, Niemöller never deviated from the uncompromising line taken at Barmen and Dahlem. Against the Reich Bishop and his "satanic despots" he waged unceasing war by every available means — in his sermons and speeches, in the press and in his private correspondence. In July, 1935, Hitler created a Ministry for Church Affairs. When the new Minister spoke of "pacification" and of "reconciling the two opposing groups", that alone was enough to ensure that Niemöller and his friends would have nothing to do with him. To them, reconciliation with the German Christians was neither possible nor desirable. In the words of a contemporary leaflet: "We share neither the same God, nor the same Faith, nor the same Inspiration." As for the neutrals, those churchmen who preferred to play the role of impartial arbitrators, Niemöller told the new Ministry bluntly that he had no confidence in men who shirked the responsibilities God laid upon them by refusing to fight.

Yet, despite his vehemence, consistency and courage, Niemöller steadily lost adherents and dissension within the Confessing Church increased until, at the fourth Synod at Bad Oynhausen in February, 1936, it seemed on the point of wrecking the organization. Once already, in the spring of 1935, Niemöller had been arrested and he and five hundred other pastors spent three days in prison for having defied the Ministry of the Interior's ban by reading a declaration from their pulpits rejecting the new paganism. In the autumn of 1936, Niemöller fully expected to be arrested again and calmly prepared for the possibility, but it was a false alarm. In the spring of 1937, he was informed that charges were pending against him for alleged treasonable utterances — on no less than forty counts. He already knew that the Public Prosecutor had for some time been collecting material.

The sands were running out. What had he achieved? Little enough. The fact was, there were too few Niemöllers. One day, he came home to lunch with news that one of his close friends had defected to the German Christians. His eleven-year-old son, Jochen, burst into tears. "Cheer up!" his father told him. "What are you crying about?" "If only there were more *men*!" said his son.

In June, 1937, the clergy who were to represent the Confessing Church at the World Conference in Oxford had their passports confiscated by the police. Shortly afterwards the majority of the leaders of the Confessing Church were arrested by the Gestapo while holding a meeting in a Berlin church. Still Niemöller remained untouched. If he was downcast, he never showed it. On one or two mornings at the end of June, he managed to spare a few minutes to visit the artist, Ludwig Bartning, who had repeatedly asked him to sit for his portrait. "We did not talk much about the immediate future," recollects Bartning. "Niemöller seemed to know he was standing on the brink. The expression in the finished portrait was more sombre than I had realized—or intended."

Chapter Six

TRIAL FOR TREASON

(1936–45)

AT half past eight on the morning of 1 July, 1937, there was a
ring at the front door of Martin Niemöller's rectory. It was
the first day of the school holidays and his two eldest sons had
already set off on their bicycles for a four weeks' tour of East
Prussia. Their mother had just come back from the railway
station where the girls, Hertha and Jutta, had gone on a trip to
the Baltic. Niemöller himself had taken a bath and, still in his
dressing-gown, was scrambling about on the nursery floor with
his youngest son, Martin, playing with a toy motor-car. He had
got home late on the previous night from a conference with
Lutheran Church leaders, in Bielefeld.

The maid-of-all-work, Dora, answered the bell. She had been
with the Niemöller family for years and so when she was confronted with two Gestapo men who asked to see her master, she
was performing no more than a familiar ritual when she showed
them into the living-room and calmly went to tell the Pastor.
Dressing quickly, Niemöller came down to his visitors. They
said they wanted to ask him a few questions—would he care to
accompany them? Niemöller went outside and got into the
Grüne Minna, as the Berliners call their version of the Black
Maria. He was not particularly disturbed. He had often been
questioned by the Gestapo and the men had told him that, this
time, the interrogation would be short. He had no need to look
through the window to know where he was being taken. As on
previous occasions, the van was heading towards East Berlin

and the huge police headquarters in the Alexanderplatz. After his late night, it was all he could do to stay awake.

Arrived at their destination, the Gestapo men took Niemöller inside and told him to wait. The expected interrogation never took place. Instead, after waiting some hours, Niemöller was told to get back into the police van and was taken to the remand prison in Moabit. There his personal particulars were recorded, all his valuables were removed and he was put in a cell. With one small window high up in the wall and a squint-hole in the door, the cell was bare except for a table, stool, mess-tin and a bed of planks hinged against the wall which, as Niemöller was repeatedly warned, might be let down and used only at night. But he was dog-tired and so, as soon as the door was shut and bolted, he lay down on the concrete floor just as he was, in coat, collar and tie and slept.

Meanwhile, some two hours after Niemöller had left with the Gestapo officers, there came another and more peremptory ring at the rectory door. When the maid opened it, she saw nine men standing outside. She knew at once who they were and what they had come for. The man nearest to her she recognized as Police Cadet Officer Chantré, a clergyman's son from the Rhineland who took particular pleasure in taunting Niemöller and his friends. Dora tried to slam the door in his face, but Chantré already had his foot in the jamb. A few moments later he had led his troop to the living-room which was filled with visitors, mostly parsons who had come to attend a meeting of the Confessing Church.

"*Heil Hitler! Meine Herren, Sie sind alle verhaftet!*" One and all were now under arrest. From time to time, further callers would arrive at the rectory, to be let in, then arrested and sent to join the others in the living-room. Before long it was packed with bewildered prisoners. Two of them began to play chess; others unable to keep still, kept pacing to and fro; the remainder talked. Then Niemöller's eleven-year-old son, Jan, seated himself at the piano and started playing and singing

This photograph of Pastor Niemöller and his son Martin ("Tini") was taken at his home in Dahlem in 1936 chorales. Only Martin remained unconcerned. Too young to understand what was happening, the child ran gleefully from one Gestapo man to another as they started ransacking the house for evidence of his father's treason.

The search continued until noon, when, leaving one of their number to guard the front door, the Gestapo men went to a nearby inn for lunch, while the rectory kitchen provided bacon and eggs for the prisoners in the living-room. After lunch the search was resumed, continuing all afternoon and evening. It was getting on for 9 p.m. when the Gestapo finally left, taking with them stacks of Niemöller's correspondence and other papers and 30,000 marks' worth of collection money belonging to the Confessing Church which they had found in a wall-safe behind a picture of Saint Peter. Before going, they set free the inmates of the living-room and now, as the clock struck the hour, the last of the clergy whispered his reassurances to Frau Niemöller and bade her good night.

Alone, Frau Niemöller thought of her husband. He had been gone over twelve hours. Where was he? Why had he not returned? She looked round at the silent house—doubly silent after the events of the day—and the answers that came to her mind filled her with dread. At that moment, she thought she heard singing—girls' voices singing very softly in the street outside. Going up to the landing she opened a window and looked out. It was the women's section of the Dahlem parish choir. They had just heard of the pastor's arrest and had come to offer their comfort.

*   *   *

The news of Niemöller's arrest attracted attention far beyond the borders of Germany. The *Deutsche Nachrichtenbüro*, the official Nazi news agency, put out a tendentious explanation, saying that Niemöller had been making inflammatory speeches inciting the populace to rebellion. "A Devilish Pastor", ran a typical Nazi headline, but there were many people both at home and abroad who were not deceived. They knew of Niemöller's courageous defence of the Christian Faith against perversion by the Nazis, they were convinced of the sincerity of his motives, and the news of his arrest provoked a storm of protest. Dr. Bell, for example, the Bishop of Chichester, wrote to *The Times*: "Dr. Niemöller is a man whom any Christian might well be proud to count as a friend. I have never seen a braver Christian, nor a man in whom the lamp of faith burns more brightly." In Niemöller's own parish, from the day after his arrest until the end of the war, intercession services were held in the smaller of the two churches, the 700-year-old church of Saint Anne, at first twice weekly and later daily, while every evening a different Berlin pastor delivered the address. Year-in, year-out, the services were well attended, especially by women who came to pray for Niemöller and for all Christians suffering for the Faith.

Only once did the Gestapo attempt to interfere with a service and that was in the summer of 1937, shortly after Niemöller had been arrested. On the Sunday in question a service of mass intercession had been planned with representatives from every parish in Berlin and the Province of Brandenburg. On the Saturday evening, too late for those attending to be warned, the Gestapo suddenly ordered the service to be cancelled. On the following afternoon, when pilgrims converged on Dahlem in their thousands, coming by bus, tram and underground, they found the doors of the huge modern church of Jesus Christ locked against them by order of the Gestapo. But no one thought of going home. Ranging themselves before the church, the crowds resisted every effort of the police to disperse them, and sang psalms interspersed with lessons from the Bible read by some of the clergy who had come with them.

Later in the afternoon the people formed up into a long column and to the lusty singing of Luther's ancient hymn: *Ein feste Burg ist unser Gott,* they marched in procession to the smaller church of Saint Anne. This also they found locked. Beside it the police had brought up a number of open lorries which they now proceeded to fill with the protesting demonstrators, driving them through the centre of Berlin to the police headquarters in the Alexanderplatz. The police had no time to pick and choose when making their arrests and amid the throng surging through the corridors, the voices that now topped all others in the shrillness of their protests were those of some innocent Sunday afternoon strollers.

The comic side of this incident should not obscure the fact that courage was required for a German citizen to take part in such a protest march, as it was to express criticism at any time under the Nazi government. Those that did so were never under any illusion as regards the risk they were running, and when they were made to suffer for their outspokenness, there was never a lack of "I-told-you-so's". This was a typical reaction to Niemöller's arrest, on the part of the clergy as well as among laymen. Nor was it difficult sometimes to detect behind the remark a note of relief that the trouble-maker would now no longer be able to disturb the somnolent calm of ecclesiastical conclaves.

Such reactions were to be expected, for brave men are never popular with the less brave. It was natural, also, for the German Christians to go further and openly rejoice at their enemy's downfall, when, disregarding the wishes of Niemöller's parishioners, the Reich Bishop suspended him "in absentia" from his appointment as Pastor of Dahlem.

Of more serious consequence to the Evangelical opposition in Germany was the unwitting support given by some distinguished foreign visitors to the Nazi policy of subordinating the Church to the State. Well meaning but gullible, these men fell an easy prey to the Nazi officials who surrounded them as soon as they arrived and remained their sole source of information for as long as they stayed in Germany. The Bishop of Gloucester, for example, was told gently but firmly that the Church was faring none too badly under the new government and would continue to prosper provided the clergy obeyed the laws of the land and steered clear of politics. Evidently the Bishop thought the proviso a reasonable one, for on his return home, he wrote to *The Times* explaining that Pastor Niemöller was very properly in prison for having meddled in matters which were none of his concern. In saying this, the Bishop was, no doubt, drawing a false analogy with the Church in England and thinking how reprehensible it would be if the vicar of one of his own parishes, say, refused to obey a particular government on the ground that he disliked its politics. But in Britain it had long been established that, whatever its politics, no government could initiate legislation on matters of Church doctrine or internal management, hence churchmen never found themselves in a position where their loyalty to the Church conflicted with the loyalty they owed to the State. In Germany it was this very principle of non-interference between Church and State which the Nazi government flouted, and for the maintenance of which Niemöller had fought and was now being made to suffer.

*   *   *

Meanwhile Niemöller was leading a tolerable existence in the remand prison in Moabit. At one time he was told that his trial would take place in August, but the date was repeatedly postponed. The weeks passed and he began to adjust himself to prison routine. Every ten days his wife was allowed to visit him, bringing one of their children with her. On her first visit she was shocked to see her husband looking pale and flaccid and her complaint ensured that thereafter he was allowed to buy five marks' worth of extra food per day. The prison doctor, a half-Jew and himself "persona non grata", proved friendly and thanks to him Niemöller was allowed to lie on his bed during the daytime and take a warm bath once a week. But these concessions could not rob his lot of its bitterness. The flagrant injustice remained, fanning his impatience until one day when the prison chaplain came to see him, he finally boiled over.

"But Brother! What brings *you* here? Why are you in prison?" asked the chaplain somewhat foolishly.

To which Niemöller replied angrily: "And Brother, why are you *not* in prison?"

Hard as it was for so vital and active a man to adjust himself to close confinement and the loss of his freedom, Niemöller was not the type to allow himself to become demoralized. A glance at the letters he wrote when he was in the remand prison show that clearly enough. It was not he who lacked courage, but he who inspired it, setting his family and friends an example of unswerving faith in God and warning them, now that most of the leaders of the Confessing Church were in prison, not to lose confidence or tire in their efforts. "I often think now of Jesus' last words to Peter," he wrote in one of his letters. " 'And another shall gird thee and lead thee whither thou willst not go.' " Perhaps even more significant was another letter which he wrote in January, 1938, after being in prison more than six months. The letter shows that his faith and confidence in the good cause were still unbroken, and it is interesting that his language still reveals the former sailor. In the letter he compared the Church with a ship that had drifted on to a sandbank: "Somehow during these six months the ship of the Church has freed itself and is floating again. The paint is peeling, the masts are broken, she is a sorry sight. But the Lord Jesus still stands at the helm and the ship is afloat!"

Answering correspondence took up a lot of Niemöller's time. For the first few weeks he could receive and send mail in unlimited quantities, but before long, as the volume of greetings and expressions of goodwill from all over the world kept on increasing and Niemöller's outgoing post swelled in proportion, the prison censors decided to limit the latter to twelve postcards a day. For each recipient Niemöller went to great pains to find a suitable Bible text. Bible study, particularly of the Old Testament as being the special target of the German Christians' abuse, also took up a good deal of his time. Most of the remainder, apart from the twenty minutes' exercise allowed him daily, he spent with his lawyers. The odd spare minutes he devoted to learning hymns by heart. When his youngest daughter, Jutta, heard of this, she decided she would learn the same hymns in her own spare time—to keep her father company.

On 14 January, 1938, his forty-sixth birthday, Niemöller was summoned to appear before the prison governor. On the floor of the governor's office stood two large crates full of birthday letters and greetings. "We shall never censor all that!" said the governor. "You had better make a selection." So Niemöller knelt down and, more or less at random, picked up an armful of mail and handed it to the governor for censoring. Those few letters he received back later in the day, but the remainder, by far the largest part of his birthday mail, he never saw again.

Meanwhile during those months Frau Niemöller and her children came to realize with joyous amazement that they were not to be abandoned in their misfortune. Whenever they were in need of advice or help, friends were ready and waiting to assist. A typical story, which Frau Niemöller particularly enjoyed telling in later years on her lecture tours, was that of the goose. One Sunday morning shortly after her husband's arrest, she opened the front door to find a fine fat goose hanging from the door-knob. The whole family were overjoyed at the unexpected treat for their Sunday dinner. Money had always been short in the large Niemöller family, but outweighing material cares was now the knowledge that they were surrounded by friends and well-wishers during this anxious time. Moreover that was only the first goose. For five successive Sundays there was a fresh bird on the door-knob for the family dinner. To this day the donor has remained anonymous.

Niemöller's trial began on 7 February, 1938, nearly seven-and-a-half months after his arrest. Throughout that time he had been in solitary confinement. Yet the indictment drawn up by the Public Prosecutor had been put in the hands of his judges in July, 1937. It comprised fourteen typewritten pages. It described Niemöller as "one of the most extreme members of the Confessing Church", and accused him of a number of offences against the laws of the Reich, in particular of having, in Berlin and in other parts of the Reich, in the years 1935 and 1936, expressed opinions before public Church gatherings, in his capacity as clergyman, on matters of exclusive concern to the State, in a manner calculated to cause a breach of the peace. The indictment specified "malicious and provocative criticism of the Minister of Propaganda and Public Enlightenment, Dr. Goebbels, of the Minister of Education, Dr. Rust, and of the Minister of Justice, Dr. Gürtner, of a kind calculated to undermine the confidence of the People in their political leaders". These charges were brought under Hitler's "Law for the Prevention of Treacherous Attacks on State and Party and for the Maintenance of Respect for Party Uniforms".

Further, the indictment accused Niemöller of having read out from his pulpit, contrary to the express order of the Reich Minister of the Interior, the names of former parishioners who had resigned their Church membership, of having publicly sought to justify such procedure and of having called upon other pastors to follow his example.

An additional charge, added to the indictment on 17 January, 1938, that is, only three weeks before the start of the trial, alleged that Niemöller had "in the course of his clerical duties disseminated written material in which matters of concern to the State were discussed or declared upon in a manner calculated to cause a breach of the peace".

The only witnesses the prosecution could find to support these charges were two junior members of the Berlin Criminal Police, who had been detailed to attend functions organized by the Confessing Church, and the Chief Constable of the Westphalian town of Bielefeld. Against them, Niemöller's three defending counsel had arrayed, by the time the trial opened, no less than forty-two persons, among them, as witnesses-to-fact, the retired Imperial Ambassador, von Kemnitz, a sister of Hermann Goering, and two senior members of the Foreign Office. Each of them had regularly attended Niemöller's church services and his parish evenings. The witnesses-to-character included Professor Sauerbruch, the famous surgeon, Ambassador Ulrich von Hassell, the O.C. North Sea Naval Base, Admiral Otto Schultze, and Lieutenant-General von Watter who had commanded the Volunteer Defence Corps in 1922.

The Special Court where the proceedings took place was in a building connected with the prison by an underground tunnel. On the morning of the day appointed, Niemöller was transferred to a cell beneath the court whence in due course he was conducted before his judges. A green-uniformed official came to escort him from his cell in the prison. Down a corridor and up a long flight of stone steps the two men walked in silence. Niemöller had no illusions about being given a fair trial. The object of trying him at all was obviously to make an example of him for the benefit of those Evangelical opponents of Hitler who were still at large. The court would be packed with his enemies. However trivial the evidence, whatever he or his counsel might say in his defence, the result of the trial was a foregone conclusion. Alone with his gaoler, their steps echoing in the stone corridors, Niemöller was suddenly filled with dread and a terrible feeling of loneliness. Where were his family, his friends? Where were the men of the Confessing Church who had fought with him for the maintenance of their common Faith?

There followed one of the strangest and most uplifting experiences of Niemöller's life. The man escorting him to the cell beneath the court-room had so far not uttered a word. His face was impassive, his footsteps regular; he was an automaton and Niemöller was barely aware of his presence. All he knew was that the man was somewhere close behind him. They had passed through the underground tunnel and were just reaching the flight of steps that, Niemöller guessed, led up to the court. He expected to be taken straight in. The judges would already be assembled. What would they do with him. . . ? He was still struggling with his fear and a sort of prayer ran through his mind. At that precise moment Niemöller heard a voice. It seemed to be repeating some set form of words, but it was so low, he was unable at first to distinguish them, and it was difficult to tell where the voice came from because of the echo. Then he realized it was his gaoler speaking, and speaking to him. What was he saying? "The Name of the Lord. . ." It was a quotation, surely, from the Bible? From *Proverbs*. Yes! "The Name of the Lord is a strong tower. The righteous runneth into it, and is safe." The voice spoke barely above a whisper. It sounded remote and expressionless. Now it had stopped. *Nomen Domini turris fortissima. . . .* Niemöller was climbing the steps now and gave no sign that he had heard. But his fear had gone, and in its place was the calm brilliance of an utter trust in God.

Once or twice during the days that followed Niemöller caught a glimpse of the gaoler's green uniform by the door on the far side of the court. But he could not see his face, and he never saw him close-to again. Almost twenty years later, on 14 January, 1957, Niemöller was confronted once more with those same words. It was his sixty-fifth birthday and among the presents was one from a woman, an anonymous well-wisher who lived in the area of the Hessen-Nassau Church, of which Niemöller was President. She had sent him a silver coin that had belonged to her family for many years. It was dated 1772 and on one side showed a silhouette of the city of Frankfurt-am-Main. Surrounding the picture were some Latin words: *Nomen Domini turris fortissima.*

The first thing he saw on entering the court was a picture of Adolf Hitler, in glaring colours, on the centre of the wall behind the judges' rostrum. Proceedings began with the ejection of all members of the general public from the court; a large crowd still awaiting admittance outside, among them the Dean of Chichester who had come as an observer on behalf of the Ecumenical Council, was turned away. Niemöller and his defending counsel protested in vain against the decision to hold the trial in camera, pointing out that such procedure was damaging to the good name of Germany, and would seem to lend support

111

to rumours, current abroad, that German Justice was no longer impartial. The Public Prosecutor refused to give way; not even the Press was admitted. The Propaganda Ministry had warned the German Press in advance that they were not to print anything about the trial except the official hand-outs.

The first day passed without major incident. Niemöller was called on to give an account of his career and did so "in simple but very effective words", as even Alfred Rosenberg's personal representative at the trial had to admit. Niemöller spoke for over three hours, stressing—naturally enough—those aspects of his life which would appeal to his Nazi judges: his aversion to any form of republican government, his initial sympathy with some of the aims of National Socialism and, above all, his record of service in the First World War, at the same time stoutly defending his attitude in the protracted Battle of the Churches. On the second day there was a sharp clash between the Public Prosecutor and the accused. The Gestapo had claimed to have received information that in some parishes in Britain the church bells had been rung as a form of intercession for Niemöller. The Gestapo also reported that the British Press seemed to be unusually well informed on the background to the trial. These statements were seized on by the prosecution as evidence that Niemöller had been maintaining treasonable relations with a foreign power, and on the pretext that such matters could be discussed only in camera, those members of Niemöller's Confessing Church who had so far been permitted to attend the trial were ordered to leave the court. Having in vain protested against this arbitrary procedure, Niemöller declared:

"Very well, in that case I refuse to testify further. I shall not speak another word at this trial and I shall take no more part in it than a living corpse. My counsel is discharged!"

The court then detailed someone else to defend Niemöller, but the latter refused him all powers to act on his behalf and would not allow him to peruse any of his files. The court was then adjourned for ten days while the prosecution cogitated the next step.

Meanwhile, at least one Nazi official attending the trial had already made up his mind on the question of Niemöller's guilt or innocence, and later declared his opinion as follows: "This trial is one of the most shameful and unworthy spectacles which I have ever witnessed . . . no reliable evidence has been forthcoming . . . such trials should not and must not be allowed to take place in Germany . . . in our opinion such methods belong to the G.P.U. . . . Germany has no voice in this. . . ."

All attempts having failed during the ten-day recess to persuade Niemöller to co-operate in his own trial, it was then resumed with the accused attending as a silent spectator and his counsel, though present, largely inactive. The remaining five days of the trial revealed an almost total lack of evidence against Niemöller. All the prosecution could produce were the "observations" of two Gestapo men who had been detailed to shadow Niemöller for some days before his arrest, whereas on Niemöller's side were ranged a large number of well known and highly respected individuals from all walks of life, every one of whom was ready to testify on his behalf. One of them, the famous surgeon, Dr. Sauerbruch, made a particularly strong impression with his courageous statement: "Would to God we had a few more such parsons in Germany!" Even before the trial ended, it was clear that the presiding judge considered it ought never to have taken place and he went out of his way to avoid calling Niemöller "the accused" because not even the semblance of a case had been made out against him.

The morning of 25 February, 1938—the last day of the trial—was taken up with another clash between prosecution and defence over the alleged bias shown by foreign press correspondents. Then Niemöller addressed the court for the last time. Speaking quietly, without trace of heat, he said that the trial sprang from the cleavage which had arisen between the new ideology and the teaching of the Church, and from the attempt

113

'to impose the one upon the other. Once again he expressed his belief that limits were set to human authority, including that of the totalitarian State; those limits were the Gospel of Jesus Christ. "The State, Mankind, the whole world," he said in conclusion, "will rob themselves of their true destiny and their ultimate goal if they fail to respect or recognize the frontier here drawn."

The findings were announced on 2 March. The public had been admitted, and when Niemöller entered the crowded courtroom at noon, he saw his wife and his eldest daughter, Brigitte, sitting in the front row. In a detailed report of the trial published two days later, the London *Daily Telegraph* described him as wearing a dark suit with wing-collar and black tie. Looking the typical German naval officer, said the newspaper, Niemöller had entered the dock smiling and confident and had warmly shaken hands with his defending counsel. The findings of the court covered fifteen typewritten pages. They reflected the judge's sympathy with the accused. Niemöller, they said, had been inspired by "completely honourable motives. The examination-in-chief has shown that he is a man of unquestionable veracity, the type of individual who has nothing whatever of the traitor in him. That he came, nevertheless, into conflict with the Law was due to special circumstances, and these are best defined in the words of a witness who said that the accused was a truly tragic example of divided loyalties."

Nevertheless, Niemöller had been tried before a Nazi court and the judges were afraid to acquit him. Instead, they sentenced him to seven months' detention in a fortress (an unusual and "honourable" form of punishment) and imposed a fine of 2000 marks. The term of detention and one quarter of the fine were remitted in recognition of the fact that he had already spent over seven months in solitary confinement. In addition to paying a fine of 1500 marks, or alternatively serving a term of three months' imprisonment, Niemöller was ordered to pay the costs of the trial. Technically, therefore, he was now a free man.

The sentence was an astonishingly light one. "There are still some judges left in Berlin" wrote the *Basler Nachrichten* when reporting the trial next day. Niemöller himself was overjoyed. "It's better than an acquittal!" he told his wife when she congratulated him. "I've no complaints!" Not so the Minister of Justice. The judges had proved poor servants of National Socialism and he blocked their further promotion forthwith.

As for Frau Niemöller, despite her relief, she could not forget the warning which a friend of the family had given her during the trial. "Whatever happens," this man had said, "they won't set him free." Now, Frau Niemöller felt in duty bound to tell her husband as soon as she could. But released from the long suspense, Niemöller was in no mood to meet further troubles half-way and, though it came from a trustworthy friend, he waved the warning aside. "I shall be home in an hour or two!" he said. Then he was led back to his cell, where he packed his bags, never doubting that that evening would see him in Dahlem again, surrounded by his family.

Late that night, after he had waited in vain for his freedom, two Gestapo officers in plain clothes took him by private car to the concentration camp at Sachsenhausen.

* * *

Lying to the north of Berlin, Sachsenhausen, even at that time, contained thirty thousand prisoners—the population of a medium-sized town. It was after 1 a.m. when Niemöller was marched through the double entrance gates and handed over to the S.S. guards. He still had no idea why he had been taken there or why he had not been released.

First, all his personal belongings were confiscated: his wedding ring and his watch, as articles of value with which he might try to bribe his guards—his Bible and the letters which his wife had written to him while he was awaiting trial, as written material which he might adapt for the purpose of conveying secret messages—and his braces. Why were they taking his braces?

115

"So you can't hang yourself," was the reply. Stripped of his possessions, Niemöller was then taken through two more pairs of gates and into the building which contained the cells. He was locked in cell No. 1.

Next morning the camp commandant, an S.S. officer by the name of Baranovsky, came to see him. He said Niemöller had been sent to Sachsenhausen as "the *Führer's* personal prisoner". "I've never had anyone in that category before," said the commandant, "and I've had no instructions yet on how to treat you. Meanwhile, have you any requests or complaints?" So Hitler had not forgotten, thought Niemöller, or forgiven him for issuing his blunt warning after the conference in January, 1934. As Hitler's own judges would not put him behind bars, the *Führer* had done so himself.

"Yes, I have got a request," Niemöller replied, and telling the commandant about the confiscation of his belongings, he asked to have his Bible back. After some bluster about "that dangerous book", Baranovsky turned to his adjutant and said: "Fetch the man his Bible. It's on the desk in my office." Some days later, Niemöller's ring, watch, letters and hymn book were also returned.

A month passed before Frau Niemöller got a letter from her husband. It was heavily censored and artificially non-committal in tone. Another month and she was allowed to visit him, not in the concentration camp but at the police headquarters in Berlin where he was taken by car with an armed guard. He himself was not informed of the purpose of the journey and thought he was on his way to freedom. From then on, they met once a month, always at the building in the Alexanderplatz and always in the presence of an armed guard.

Each time, Frau Niemöller was allowed to bring one of the children with her, so that Niemöller saw them all once in seven months. The interviews lasted half an hour, or forty minutes if the guard chose to be lenient. Though Church affairs and politics were forbidden topics, there was always more than enough to talk about and so that they should not forget something of importance, Niemöller and his wife took to jotting down the points for discussion before each interview.

On the outbreak of war in 1939, the meetings in Berlin were suspended and Frau Niemöller thereafter went to Sachsenhausen to see her husband. Though she could visit him once a fortnight instead of monthly, she was no longer allowed to take one of the children with her. The first time she set foot inside the concentration camp, she was surprised to find it almost attractive. There were neat gardens with beds of flowers, a stream spanned by a rustic bridge—even a lake with swans. These adornments were not planned for the benefit of the prisoners, but to mislead foreign visitors. The waiting-room into which Frau Niemöller was shown, on the other hand, was bare and ugly. Whenever she entered it, she would find women dressed in mourning, waiting, as she later discovered, to collect the urn with the ashes of some relative murdered by the S.S. guards.

For the first eighteen months of his solitary confinement, Niemöller's diet consisted largely of bread and potatoes. Occasionally, he managed to get extras from the canteen, such as chocolate, but on each successive visit, his wife found him thinner and paler and she became increasingly concerned. She tried to conceal her anxiety from her children, but one day, after visiting the camp and finding that her husband's eyesight was beginning to fail, she could no longer contain herself and told the children that their father was being slowly starved to death. A few days later, Frau Niemöller was summoned by the Gestapo. They told her, she ought not to tell lies to her children about conditions at Sachsenhausen. For some time she was at a loss to think of the source of the Gestapo's information. Then the truth came out. Her daughter, Hertha, had told her school friends of her father's ill treatment and one of them had written an indignant letter of protest to Hitler. Strangely enough, however, it produced the desired result. Some days later, the S.S. guard who brought Niemöller his midday bowl of gruel, produced instead a complete meal consisting of soup, cutlet, potatoes and brussels-sprouts.

"Orders from higher authority," said the man. "From now on you're to have double S.S. rations." Niemöller set to ravenously. Within a few days, the worst of his hunger had been satisfied and thereafter he secretly gave half his midday dinner to a fellow prisoner whose job it was to go round the cells collecting the empty soup bowls. The man was a member of that courageous sect, the Jehovah Witnesses.

From the moment he crossed the threshold of Sachsenhausen as Hitler's personal prisoner, Niemöller's presence there was kept a close secret, even from the other prisoners. He was woken before reveille in the mornings, made to exercise alone and when he had to go to the dentist outside the camp, he was taken in the hearse or in a wheel-barrow. Nevertheless, he managed to establish contact with his fellow prisoners.

"I was in solitary confinement," Niemöller told a post-war audience in Philadelphia. "I was not supposed to talk to anyone. But my cell had a window and on the second morning after I had been sent to Sachsenhausen, I heard footsteps outside, then more steps—a whole party of people. I pushed my table to the wall, put the stool on top, climbed up and looked out. There I saw about fifteen prisoners, one behind the other, taking their morning exercise round the grass in the courtyard. Next morning, and after that, every morning, I climbed on to my stool as soon as I heard the footsteps outside and called out just loud enough for the men to hear a text from the Holy Bible, sometimes from the Old Testament, sometimes from the New. In that way, Hitler achieved something he certainly never intended—the Word of God had found a voice in the very Gates of Hell."

On another occasion, Niemöller explained how he had managed to make himself heard by the other prisoners but not by the guards. He had acquired the art of talking from one corner of his mouth, he said. By the autumn of 1938 he had long since perfected this technique and one day he read Mass to a prisoner as the latter was weeding a flower-bed outside his window. The man was a Catholic priest.

Executions in the camp were not uncommon and sometimes Niemöller heard shots coming from the direction of the cells. More than once he saw a corpse hung up beside the main road in the camp as a warning to the unwary. There were other and worse atrocities which Niemöller has preferred to forget. "You ask, what was it like?" he said to an American audience in 1945. "Was it really as bad as all that? I can only reply: yes, it was —and a thousand times worse."

On two occasions during his captivity, Niemöller saw his father. In 1940, the old man was allowed to visit him in the camp. He was nearing eighty-one and had celebrated his golden wedding anniversary in the previous year. The reward for his long and exhausting journey from the Rhineland to Berlin was thirty minutes with his son in a bleak waiting-room. Before they parted, Heinrich Niemöller put his hands on his son's shoulders and said in his deep, soothing voice: "My dear boy, have no fear! The Eskimos in North Canada and the Bataks in Sumatra send their greetings and want you to know you are in their prayers."

A year later, on the evening of 17 March, 1941, Martin Niemöller was given leave to spend an hour with his father. While four Gestapo officers patrolled the house to prevent the prisoner from contacting the outside world, a fifth stationed himself behind a screen in the room where Heinrich Niemöller was dying. The old man had not lost his sense of humour. "Give the poor chap a cigar," he said to his wife, "but not one of the black ones!" The black ones were the best. As Heinrich talked with his son, the sorrow of their last reunion turned to a sense of comfort, almost of joy. His last words were those of Jacob in the Bible, and he addressed them particularly to Martin. "Behold, I die. But God shall be with you." That same night, Martin had to leave his mother and return to the concentration camp.

Shrouded in his old cassock, Heinrich Niemöller was buried in Elberfeld in the presence of large numbers of his former parishioners. A last minute ban imposed by the Gestapo was powerless to prevent a colleague of Martin's in the fight against Hitler from preaching the sermon, and the inscription of his own choice on the tomb where Heinrich Niemöller was laid to rest in company with those who had preceded him as pastors of the parish, spoke not only comfort, but also a challenge: "THE WORD OF THE LORD ENDURETH FOR EVER."

* * *

Not long after his father's death, on the Thursday of Easter week, Martin Niemöller was being escorted down the main road of the camp towards the administration building, where a visitor was waiting to see him. The way led past a hut in which some hundreds of pastors were being held prisoner, among them Niemöller's friend, the Berlin pastor, Heinrich Grüber. Grüber had been given the job of keeping the verges of the road in good order and as he walked past, Niemöller saw that his friend had scratched in the gravel the Latin word: *VIVIT*—HE LIVES. The Easter Message deeply engraved in the soil of Sachsenhausen! Who can say what comfort it spelt to the prisoners who saw it, on how many personal failures and capitulations it set the seal of pardon? For all prisoners had their moments of despair and it was in one such moment, perhaps, in September, 1941, that Niemöller had written to Grand Admiral Raeder asking to be recalled for service in the German Navy. As soon as the letter had left his hands, Niemöller regretted it and succeeded in getting it back, but when she next visited him, his wife persuaded him to post it again.

As might have been foreseen, the application was refused. For once already, in May, 1938, Raeder had made it clear that he considered Niemöller deserved to be in prison. The German Pastors' Union had asked him to approach Hitler with a view to obtaining Niemöller's release. Raeder replied: "I regret that

I cannot, on principle, concern myself with the affairs of Pastor Niemöller seeing that his past actions have inflicted so much harm on the Evangelical Church." Now Raeder left it to Field-Marshal Keitel to reply. The latter wrote in a more courteous strain, addressing the letter to "Lieutenant Commander Niemöller (Retd.)".

"In reply to your application of 7 September, I regret to have to inform you that it is not intended to recall you for active service in the Navy. Heil Hitler!"

There, for the time being, the matter rested. It was reopened after the war when violent controversy arose concerning Niemöller's motive in applying to fight in Hitler's war. Mrs. Roosevelt, and with her many of his religious and political opponents, went so far as to accuse him of defecting to the Nazi cause. The Swiss psychologist, C. G. Jung, considered that the incident could only be explained in terms of psycho-pathology. In a letter to the American magazine, *News Week*, Niemöller himself said that he had been prompted solely by the desire to resume active opposition to Hitler. It seems moreover that his decision to write the letter was chiefly due to the persuasion of friends. "We talked him over," asserts Niemöller's friend and former parishioner, the artist, Professor Ludwig Bartning. "And after long argument, he agreed." Bartning was no doubt right in detecting a higher logic in the rejection of Niemöller's application. "He was not to be allowed to bear arms in an unjust war under the most unjust of all 'Leaders'. We ought to have realized that, instead of trying to gain petty advantages for him. It confirmed what I already knew: it is wrong even to want to give Niemöller advice. He possesses an indestructible instinct for what is true and just. It does not amount to omniscience, but it is sure and sound, and he acts accordingly."

*   *   *

When it became known in March, 1938, that Martin Niemöller had been thrust into a concentration camp despite his acquittal by a Nazi court, a storm of protest arose from every corner of Germany. The request of the German Pastors' Union to Grand Admiral Raeder struck a note which was echoed in many places. In a declaration addressed to the Minister of Justice, 362 theologians from Niemöller's home province of Westphalia affirmed their support for his cause. Nearly 3000 pastors who were members of the Confessing Church signed a petition for his release. The Gestapo Headquarters in Berlin, the Ministry of Justice, the Reich Chancellory itself were besieged by deputations of private citizens with the same object. Yet further proof was forthcoming that Martin Niemöller had not been forgotten. A year after he had been sent to the concentration camp, an anonymous book was published in Switzerland entitled *Martin Niemöller and his Creed*. The book attracted much attention at the time, but it was not until some years later that its authorship was revealed. It had been written by Niemöller's former curate in Dahlem, Dr. Franz Hildebrandt.

These proofs of devotion to himself and his cause, as far as he came to know them, gave Niemöller good reason for satisfaction. Yet, the longer his captivity lasted, the greater became his concern for the future of the Evangelical Church. Most of the leaders of the Confessing Church were already behind bars. Robbed of their pastors, many parishes were weakening in their resistance to the demands of the German Christians. The opposition to Hitler, which had been built up with so much difficulty, was in process of crumbling—and needless to say, the German Christians were showing no inclination to step into the breach. What a contrast, thought Niemöller, with the impressive unity of the Roman Catholic Church! Here was no bargaining, no jockeying for position, no "co-existence with National Socialism."

Thus, perhaps, Niemöller argued, alone in his cell in Sachsenhausen, disillusioned, weary and tending to idealize the characteristics of the Catholic Church in Germany, which he knew only from the outside, by contrast with the drab and dispiriting internal squabbles of his own. Whether or not this was the process of his thought, the fact remains that, starting some time in 1940, the letters which he wrote from the concentration camp became strongly Catholic in tone—so much so that, on the strength of Niemöller's unmistakable change of attitude, some of his close friends became converted to Catholicism. As for his wife, she came away from her visits to him convinced that he was on the brink of doing the same. She herself had no intention of becoming a Catholic and on one occasion she asked Niemöller in desperation: "But that will mean a divorce! Do you want to divorce me?" Her husband had made no reply. Frau Niemöller then asked certain theological friends to intervene, but their arguments proved unavailing. Only the warning of a friendly priest made Niemöller pause. The priest told him that a man in captivity had no right to make decisions of such far-reaching importance, for that which suited his needs as a prisoner might lose its attraction once he was free. The priest reminded Niemöller of Frederick the Great's remark to his officers: "If I should happen to be taken prisoner, any orders I give you must be disobeyed!"

When the rumour reached Nazi ears that Niemöller was about to enter the Catholic Church there was jubilation. Here, they thought, was an opportunity to discredit him finally and present his year-long resistance to Hitler and the German Christians as mere truculence and opportunism. By March, 1941, the Nazi Press was already proclaiming his conversion as an accomplished fact. When the news was found to be premature, the Nazis seemed to think it was time they helped Niemöller to make up his mind. Accordingly in July, 1941, they transferred him to Dachau, 350 miles from Sachsenhausen, in southern Germany. Travelling with him in the open car were three fellow-prisoners, all of whom were well-known Catholic prelates. On arrival at the concentration camp, the four men were given separate cells in which to sleep, but shared a communal living-room.

In due course, Frau Niemöller was informed that her husband had been transferred to Dachau for administrative reasons. In the course of her visits there she found him greatly changed. Far from hastening his conversion to Rome, as his captors had intended, his enforced intimacy with three learned Catholics was producing the opposite result. In discussion Niemöller began to realize as never before the width of the gulf that lay between his own Faith and that of Roman Catholicism and he was now well on his way to regaining confidence in his Protestant beliefs. With his spiritual wounds healing, his wife found him looking fitter and more cheerful. He had regained his zest for life. The progressive enfeeblement she had noticed in him in Sachsenhausen had been halted, and now innumerable small signs told her that his vital energies were on the mend. The fact was, of course, that in giving him someone to talk to and argue with, the Nazis had done Niemöller the best possible service. In the company of his fellow men, his whole being expanded and already he was regaining that combination of physical health and mental vigour that had made him so formidable a protagonist in the Battle of the Churches. Behind the wasted frame and sunken eyes, the old implacable Niemöller could be seen, the man of whom the Protestant Bishop of Berlin, Dr. Dibelius, spoke in January, 1957, on the occasion of Niemöller's sixty-fifth birthday: "In him Hitler rightly discerned the very core of the Evangelical opposition, for here, if ever, was the living embodiment of that quality which the Nazis called *Kompromisslosigkeit*—the 'negation of compromise'."

Meanwhile, in 1941, during Niemöller's silence, another voice in Germany was speaking no less implacably in defence of the Christian Faith. It was the voice of the Catholic Bishop of Münster, the late Cardinal Count von Galen. Like Niemöller, a Westphalian, von Galen never minced his words and during the Nazi period his sermons were often taken down verbatim and secretly passed from hand to hand. No doubt for fear of international repercussions, Hitler had thought it wiser not to arrest

him. Soon after Niemöller's transfer to the concentration camp
at Dachau, von Galen preached a sermon in which he paid
public tribute to him in words of great courage and generosity.

> "The name of one who risked his life for Germany as a U-boat
> Commander in the First World War, and who later worked in
> Münster as an Evangelical pastor, is well known to you all. For
> years past this man has been robbed of his freedom—that also
> you know. And I say we all have the very greatest respect for this
> noble man, for his bravery and courage in bearing witness to his
> Faith."

As far as Niemöller personally was concerned, existence in
Dachau was in many respects more comfortable than in the previous camp. He continued to share a living-room with his
Roman Catholic colleagues. They were given adequate food and
Niemöller was allowed to receive books and, occasionally,
magazines. With the aid of the latter he was able to identify
some famous figures among the new arrivals in the camp: Dr.
Schuschnigg, the former Austrian Chancellor, Léon Blum, former Socialist Prime Minister of France, and Dr. Schacht,
Hitler's one-time Economic Minister, now paying the penalty
for having tried to preserve order amid Nazi financial chaos. In
due course two British officers, Best and Stevens, also arrived,
having been lured on to German soil from Holland and then
arrested by the Gestapo.

The time which he was spending in the close company of three
Catholic theologians was to prove of immense value to Niemöller. At any or all times of day, in serious argument or easy
discussion they were free, as only captives can be, to learn the
tenets of each other's faith. Moreover, their common lot and the
very necessity imposed on them of living peaceably together ensured that their arguments never overstepped the bounds of
courtesy and restraint. In this way Niemöller gained a real insight into Roman Catholicism which he had certainly never
possessed before, and in return he gave his friends a new understanding of his own Faith. And friends they were, propounding

their beliefs, not proselytizing, and intellectually honest as befitted men who had lost all freedom except the freedom to think. Every day all four prayed together from the Catholic Breviary and every day Niemöller expounded to his three colleagues a passage from the Bible. He read the Bible through five times during those years, from the first word to the last.

It was not merely his knowledge of theology which Niemöller improved during his captivity. While he was in Dachau, he read more than four hundred English books, published mostly in America, thus acquiring an excellent knowledge of the language which was to be of great use to him at post-war international religious gatherings, as well as on his lecture tours in the United States. Considerable will-power was required to pursue these concentrated studies when it is remembered that their background was nothing less than approaching national disaster. To call it Hitler's war did not alter the fact that Hitler's defeat would also be Germany's and in the final collapse of Naziism the entire national life would suffer an eclipse, although perhaps only temporarily. To devote long hours to study under the shadow of this impending disaster was difficult, and doubly so in that Niemöller and his friends had every reason to believe that, before the end finally came, they themselves would fall victims to a firing squad. Moreover in 1944 and 1945 two personal tragedies occurred in Niemöller's life. Shortly before Christmas in 1944, his youngest daughter, Jutta, died suddenly, two days after contracting diphtheria. The news was given him by one of the S.S. guards—casually, almost. It was totally unexpected. Niemöller had not known even that she was ill. Two months later, in February, 1945, his eldest son, Hans Jochen, was killed by a Russian tank not far from the North German town of Stargard, in Pomerania.

Jochen had been studying theology at Marburg University at the time of his call-up. He had then had a long illness. When in hospital in Berlin he had taken an active part in the underground movement against Hitler. He seemed to have had a premonition of his death, for before he was sent to the front he wrote a letter to his mother, entrusting it to his sister, Hertha, and telling her to deliver it only upon news that he had been killed. Owing to the chaos then prevailing in Germany, the news took a month to reach his family. One passage in the letter read: "Don't be too unhappy. I am not dying for an ideology or for an idolized Fatherland. I am dying in accordance with God's Holy Will and in fulfilment of my duty as a German. Do not quarrel with God—we are all His."

Meanwhile, Frau Niemöller had moved to the small village of Leoni in Bavaria so as to be nearer her husband. She went to Dachau to break the news of their son's death to him personally, taking two of their children with her in the belief that their presence might help to soften the blow. But the S.S. guards refused to allow them into the camp and all they could do was to wave to their father from the gate.

Niemöller's son had died fighting the advancing Russians on German soil. The tide of battle had turned. East and west the Allied grip was tightening. Hitler, the Nazi Party, his Gauleiters, his functionaries were doomed, and with them the whole machine of terror and intimidation with which they had prolonged their misrule. No one in Germany could have any doubt that the end of the war was in sight. In the concentration camp at Dachau, the S.S. officers and guards were daily becoming more unpredictable in their attitude to the prisoners, veering between leniency and redoubled harshness, as their own approaching end inspired them with fear or spite. Throughout Niemöller's captivity, for example, they had never yet allowed him to hold a religious service. His repeated requests had met with the unvarying answer: "No. The Catholics can hold their Mass because they keep to a set form of words. But with you Protestants, there is no knowing what you might say." Then, at Christmas, 1944, an unheard-of concession was made.

One afternoon in Christmas week, the S.S. officer on duty summoned the fifteen "special" prisoners, among them, Niemöller, and told them there would be no Christmas tree for them this year and they would not be permitted—as they had been on previous occasions—to sing Christmas carols. Instead, they would be allowed out of their cells for a few minutes to exchange greetings. That was all. This was a severe disappointment, particularly for the eight Protestant prisoners. They were about to return to their cells when the seventy-two-year-old former Dutch Minister of War, Dr. Van Dyck, said to the officer: "I have been here four years and we have never yet been allowed to hold a service. Please, won't you make an exception, this once?" Strangely enough, the S.S. officer agreed. "After all," he said, "what difference does it make?" So that Christmas, Niemöller held a service for the first time in nearly eight years. The congregation consisted of six men: Dr. Van Dyck, a British Indian Army colonel, two Norwegian shipowners, a Yugoslav diplomat and a Greek journalist. Niemöller preached a Christmas sermon and then celebrated Holy Communion. Before leaving Dachau, he was allowed to hold another five services for the same men. Admittedly, they came from differing Protestant denominations, but as Niemöller said in one of his sermons: "Theological differences have become so fine that today one would have to possess a more than average schooling in philosophy to be able to detect them, and if salvation depended on that ability, then only learned men could enter Heaven—a situation in clear contradiction with the teaching of Jesus."

In southern Germany the spring of 1945 was unusually warm and fine. On 21 April, Frau Niemöller went by car to Dachau to see her husband. She found the camp in turmoil. In the administration building, typewriters were being packed, drawers emptied, files removed. Outside, a column of motorized transport was being loaded with gear. She was allowed only a few minutes with her husband. He looked harassed. "They are going to move us," he said, "—drag us off somewhere. . . ." Nobody knew where or when. She left, promising to try to contact her husband again before the move took place.

Days passed and Frau Niemöller heard no more. Then she telephoned the camp: there was no reply. Next morning a friend telephoned to say that Dachau had been evacuated. The prisoners were being marched south. They were passing the village of Leoni at that very moment. It was some distance to the main road. Fortunately Niemöller's daughter, Hertha, was at home and had her bicycle. She set off at once as fast as she could for the main road. And there she saw them—hundreds of cadaverous-looking prisoners in striped jackets and trousers, lying in a meadow beside the road, watched over by their S.S. guards. Some of the villagers had brought bread and cigarettes and were hovering about, awaiting a chance to slip them to the prisoners behind the backs of the guards. They helped Hertha to look for her father—but in vain. Then she learnt that he was not with the column. Some days previously he had been among a party of 150 prisoners who were taken southwards by lorry. Where to? One of the S.S. guards told Hertha furtively—to the mountains of the Austrian Tyrol.

When she heard this news, Frau Niemöller almost abandoned hope. Both the reason for the journey and its object were all too clear. Hitler's special prisoners knew too much and he was determined to prevent them falling into Allied hands. Rather than that he would have them liquidated.

Chapter Seven

COLLAPSE OF GERMANY

(1945)

AFTER dark on the evening of 24 April, 1945, three days after Frau Niemöller's last visit to her husband in Dachau, 150 selected prisoners were bundled into open trucks and transported southwards towards an unknown destination. The party included Generals von Halder, von Falkenhausen and Thomas who had been arrested for their complicity in the July Plot, a number of women and children, victims of Hitler's vendetta against the conspirators' families, Dr. Schacht, the former President of the Reichsbank, and Martin Niemöller.

The journey continued through the night, at first in darkness and then by the light of the waning moon. In front beside the driver of Niemöller's truck sat three S.S. men armed with pistols and tommy-guns. Somewhere near Munich they passed an airfield with line upon line of Germany's latest jet-propelled aircraft, ready to fly but grounded for lack of fuel. Leaving the city on their left, they headed now towards Rosenheim and the foothills of the Alps. Wedged in beside Niemöller was Colonel von Bonin, former head of the Operations Branch of the General Staff, now convicted for having refused to carry out Hitler's order to counter-attack after the Russian capture of Warsaw. As the truck began to climb up towards Rosenheim, von Bonin whispered in Niemöller's ear: "I've got a pistol with three rounds in my pocket. Before we reach the town, I'll despatch those three in front there. Then we can tell the driver to take us back to the Danube, to the Americans." At first the idea seemed tempting, but as the pros and cons flashed through Niemöller's brain, he began to like it less. He thought of the S.S. men — perhaps they had not volunteered, but had been conscripted into the S.S. Certainly they would have families, wives and mothers waiting for them at home. Apart from that, the success of von Bonin's plan would depend largely on luck. Niemöller discussed it with him in an undertone. Could the prisoners be sure of meeting the Americans, or would they reach the Danube only to find the S.S. still there? And what about the drivers of the other trucks? If they were armed, there would be a mass slaughter. . . . Action was postponed.

In Rosenheim the trucks branched right for Innsbruck. Soon after daylight they stopped and the prisoners were put into an empty Labour Service camp on an island on the River Inn. For two days and nights they were kept there in ignorance of the fate reserved for them, while they were fed from supplies of food brought from Dachau. To pass the time and divert their thoughts from nerve-racking conjectures, the prisoners set about disposing of the armies of fleas and bed-bugs which they found in the huts. Only the S.S. officer in charge, a man by the name of Stiller, knew their destination and the ultimate purpose of the journey. Soon after the journey was resumed, the party was joined by another and more senior S.S. officer and three grim-faced men from the concentration camp at Buchenwald. The prisoners began to fear the worst.

The column of trucks continued southwards towards the Brenner Pass. A mile or more before they reached it, the road was found to be blocked with German troops who were pouring back from the Italian front, and the prisoners had perforce to wait. The sight that met their eyes seemed the very symbol of defeat: a vast throng of battle-weary men struggling up towards the head of the pass, while guns, tanks and transport stood out like dark rocks lapped by the human tide. Some of the men were empty-handed, others bunched under a load of cumbersome equipment, a few still looked fresh, almost light-hearted, as though they were glad that this was the end of Hitler's war. . . .

At length the S.S. drivers found room to move slowly forward. Crossing the Brenner, they continued for the rest of that day and on through the night. On the following morning they turned off the main road and started to descend into the valley, the idyllic Pustertal. There, near the small town of Villabassa, they stopped and the prisoners were allowed to wash themselves in a stream. As they were doing so, they saw a party of German troops coming towards them on foot. The generals identified them as the personnel of a divisional headquarters. Presumably they had run out of fuel and had had to abandon their transport. The prisoners realized at once the possibilities of the encounter. There was never much love lost between the Wehrmacht and the S.S. and these men might well be prepared to take the prisoners under their protection.

While Niemöller and others diverted the attention of the S.S. guards, von Halder and his colleagues managed to buttonhole the senior officer in the Wehrmacht party and explain the prisoners' plight, with the result that the officer promised to contact with all speed the German Chief of Staff in Italy, General von Vietinghoff-Scheel, tell him that important prisoners from Dachau, including women and children, faced imminent liquidation at the hands of Hitler's S.S. and seek full powers to ensure their safety. Soon the men of the divisional headquarters passed out of the prisoners' sight beyond the town and the latter summoned all their powers of self-control to wait patiently for the promised assistance.

For the rest of that day, the S.S. guards stayed with their prisoners in Villabassa. At nightfall they gave them some bales of straw and told them to settle themselves for the night on the floor of the empty Town Hall. Then—a clear sign of their crumbling morale—the S.S. officers raised no objection when some of the prisoners began to wander about the town. Accordingly, Niemöller, Generals von Halder, von Falkenhausen and Thomas, and Colonel von Bonin repaired to one of the local

German hotels, assured of a welcome from the South Tyrolese who had never forgiven Hitler for sacrificing their interests under his pact of friendship with Mussolini, while the S.S. officers went in search of the best Tyrolean wines elsewhere.

Some hours later, when Niemöller and his friends were comfortably installed in the bar of the *Deutsches Haus,* their fellow-prisoner from Dachau, Major Best, suddenly burst into the room. While the S.S. officer, Sturmbannführer Stiller, was deep in the mists of alcohol, he had taken the opportunity to examine his brief-case. There he had found an interesting document.... Pausing to unfold a sheet of paper, Major Best showed it to the others: an order from Himmler that none of the prisoners from Dachau was to be allowed to fall into the hands of the Americans alive....

They had thought as much. Concentrating all their hopes on the German Army officer fulfilling his promise, the prisoners meanwhile saw their greatest danger in any needless provocation of their S.S. guards. Clouded with alcohol and impatient to have done with their grisly task, the latter might all too easily resolve to carry it out on the spot. While Best was awaiting his chance to return the document to Stiller's brief-case, Niemöller and his companions thought it advisable to go back to the Town Hall and pretend to sleep—but not before arranging a system of watches so that there should be no unpleasant surprises in the night. But the night passed without incident.

Early in the morning two days later, a motorized company of German infantry drove into the town. The commanding officer, Captain von Alvensleben, had orders to release the prisoners from Dachau. In battle formation, as though besieging an enemy strongpoint, the troops encircled the Town Hall and the twelve S.S. men were ordered to come out. Meekly they obeyed, and stood in a group, awaiting further orders. Captain von Alvensleben had thoughtfully brought extra transport with him. Now he pointed to an empty truck and, turning to the S.S. men, said briefly: "Clear out of here. And don't come back!" The speed with which they obeyed showed that the S.S. men had been expecting a worse fate. Without a word they clambered into the truck and set off in the direction of Bolzano. The Captain watched them go, then, turning, saw three S.S. men standing stiffly to attention. "What do you want?" They wanted to place themselves under the protection of the German Army.

The long nightmare had ended, and with such surprising suddenness that it was some time before the prisoners awoke to the fact that they were indeed free to move about as they chose, talk to whom they pleased and, above all, take thought for their future with the knowledge that they had regained at any rate some freedom of action. Their freedom was still only relative. Caught in the midst of a retreating army, they might yet fall victim to the violence engendered by defeat and political upheaval. As an organization the S.S. was still very much alive and in an hour or two their late captors might return with reinforcements. Only the advent of the Americans could banish all possibility of a violent end.

Meanwhile two of the ex-prisoners from Dachau, an Italian and a Russian Air Force officer alleged to be Molotov's nephew, had hoisted the Italian flag over the Town Hall. The Russian had had frostbite in both his feet and so no doubt had cause to celebrate the end of his captivity—and double cause if only he had known it, for in the early hours of that same morning Adolf Hitler had committed suicide.

That night there was a heavy fall of snow and it became essential to find proper shelter for the women and children. In the event, the whole party of 150 ex-prisoners transferred to a hotel about six miles from the town. By the time the march was over, they were enormously hungry. However, the foraging party that had gone on ahead returned with a whole carcase of veal, enough to feed them all for two days. As for their thirst—someone managed to unearth, heaven knows where, one hundred bottles of brandy. Thus provided, the strange, polyglot party

Throughout the Second World War Niemöller was Hitler's personal prisoner. This photograph was taken at Pragser Wildsee in the Tyrol in May, 1945, and shows the pastor with one of the American soldiers who ultimately freed him lived for a few days under the protection of Captain von Alvensleben's field-grey uniforms. For a brief interval, tension relaxed and the survivors of Nazi liquidation talked in the seclusion of the country hotel, wandered about the grounds or sat in silence, happy to be able to surrender at last to the stupor of exhaustion.

Amongst the German troops in the area, military discipline was now rapidly disintegrating. The streets of Villabassa were swarming with soldiers intent only on laying their hands on civilian clothes preparatory to setting out, each man for himself, towards their homes in all parts of Germany. Among them Niemöller recognized a former missionary from the Neu-Kölln district of Berlin. Neither of them had any idea what the city would look like if they ever saw it again. Of one thing, at any rate, they could be certain: it would have little resemblance to the Berlin they remembered.

On 3 May, the fall of snow having meanwhile melted, units of the American Seventh Army arrived. While the men of their German bodyguard were marched off to captivity, the prisoners underwent a second liberation. They soon saw that the German and American soldiers' style of living differed as night from day. The Americans did not seem to think much of spartan living; even in war they preferred to retain some creature comforts, and the most impressive to the former inmates of Dachau was a travelling bath-house, complete with hot showers, soap and towels. You left your clothes at one end, had a shower and were given a complete new outfit from U.S. Army stocks at the other. Thus the prisoners saw the last of their striped, convict garb. For a few days then the Americans fed them with all they could eat and asked them questions about their experiences in Nazi Germany. The time went quickly, particularly for Niemöller, who had much to discuss with the U.S. Army chaplain and was also holding evening services again. After a week, however, with no signs of a move, the novelty began to wear off and the prisoners became impatient to get home to Germany. One morning the rumour got around that the ex-Dachau party was being sent south, to Verona. Yes, it was true, said the American general when Niemöller protested. No, he could do nothing about it. He had his orders.

So a column of twenty-eight command-cars took the 150 ex-prisoners to Verona. Thence, on the following day, they were transported by air to Naples where they were put in charge of the British. They were excellently cared for and the commanding officer, a brigadier, had a special surprise in store for Niemöller: a young man who, years before, had been his confirmation candidate in Dahlem, who had subsequently emigrated to the United States and was now a First Lieutenant in the U.S. Army.

At any other time, Niemöller would have relished the chance to visit Naples at the beginning of summer, but now he had only one wish: to get back to Germany as soon as he could and return to his family after a separation that had lasted nearly eight years. Meanwhile, he could appreciate that his liberators did not wish to let him go without first hearing in detail about conditions in Dachau and his own personal experiences, both as a prisoner and in his Evangelical battle against Hitler. He managed to survive press interviews and innumerable foregatherings, social and otherwise. He went to see Field-Marshal Alexander in Caserta and at his request gave his political adviser, an American, his opinions on the Allied administration of Germany. He recommended that before German political parties were revived, local government should be gradually handed over to the Germans for a trial period until they proved themselves ready for greater responsibilities. In the time that remained Niemöller and Major Stevens explored Pompeii and other nearby places of interest. For these trips his hosts generously put a jeep at his disposal.

A week passed with these activities and still there was no sign of the Germans being allowed to go home. Two weeks passed. Three weeks. A month—and the only fresh news of his family that Niemöller had heard since his wife's last visit to him in

136

Dachau, was a note from the monitoring service in Naples to say that his son, Jan, who had been taken prisoner on the eastern front in 1944, had been reported by Moscow Radio to be alive and well. At last, after five weeks in Naples, Niemöller was flown home to Germany. At Versailles the aircraft landed to pick up the former industrialist, Flick, who had at one time lived in Niemöller's parish of Dahlem, and Albert Speer, the ex-Reich Minister of Armament and War Production. Before many months were out, both were to be arraigned before the Nürnberg Tribunal as war criminals. Niemöller took only passing note of his fellow passengers, for his thoughts were concentrated on home and the prospect that before nightfall, or at the latest by the following day, he would be with his family in Bavaria. How would the Americans help him to get to Munich, he wondered. Would they send him by plane or by car?

In the event the Americans did neither. The plane landed at Wiesbaden and, escorted by an American lieutenant, Niemöller was taken by car to a villa in Wiesbaden. Before a gate opened and the car drove through, he caught a glimpse of barbed wire and the words "Interrogation Centre" on a big notice board. Without further explanation, Niemöller was then shown to a bedroom in the villa and left to his own devices. He felt angry and bitterly disappointed. Was this his reward for containing himself in patience during five weeks of questioning and interviews? If only he could see the C.O. of this interrogation centre —he felt just in the mood. But apparently the C.O. would not be available until morning, so meanwhile Niemöller asked the courteous lieutenant if it would be possible for him to get hold of a jeep and take Niemöller to see his married sister in Frankfurt. At least, then, one member of his family would know where he was. "It's a pleasure," said the lieutenant. He got hold of a jeep and drove Niemöller to Frankfurt. It was dawn before they returned.

Next morning, the commanding officer of the Interrogation Centre tried to make a scene over Niemöller "absenting himself without leave". This was the last straw. Eight years of being pushed around, then "liberation", so-called, and five weeks later, Niemöller was being lectured on good order and military discipline. He'd had enough. He wasn't playing this sort of game. He wasn't answering any more questions. "I have only this to say—I shall eat no more food until I am free to go home to my wife and family. I shall go on hunger strike." Then he added sarcastically: "And it won't be the first time. They taught us how to do without food in Dachau."

Niemöller was as good as his word. From then on, he stayed in bed and refused to eat. At lunch-time the commanding officer came personally to plead with him. At tea-time he returned, and he came again to invite him to dinner. All to no avail. "I shall eat no more until you let me go," said Niemöller. That was on a Monday. On Tuesday the pantomime was repeated—still Niemöller refused to eat. On Wednesday, forty-eight hours after his hunger-strike had started, he was still refusing; and at tea-time he refused again. Late that afternoon, the American officer came into Niemöller's bedroom and said simply: "You can go home." But "home" was in the village of Leoni where Niemöller's wife had moved to be near him in Dachau, and Leoni was some hundred miles away in Upper Bavaria at the opposite end of the American Zone. To get there Niemöller would need a sheaf of papers and passes from Military Government. Accordingly that same evening he travelled to Frankfurt. Next day, after a brief interview with General Eisenhower's political adviser, he obtained the necessary documents and by afternoon he was on his way to Bavaria in a car loaned by the President of the Frankfurt Chamber of Commerce, accompanied by his old friend, the Berlin pastor, Hans Asmussen, whom he had happened to meet in Frankfurt.

With American military transport blocking the roads, progress was slow and it was nearly midnight before they were approaching the Danube. In pouring rain and with no signposts to guide them, they were beginning to wonder whether they had lost their way, when they were suddenly caught in the head-lights of a military car. Closing to within a few yards of the Germans, the driver stopped and an American sergeant got out, followed by two somewhat tipsy G.I.s. Apparently the sight of a civilian vehicle on the road long after curfew had aroused their suspicions, for the sergeant now demanded to see the Germans' papers. Handing them out, Niemöller watched as the sergeant turned his back to the driving rain and bent down to try to decipher them under the headlights of his car. Thinking to help the man, Niemöller now descended and went up to him. It seemed the sergeant had just managed to make out the name. Suddenly his head came up and he said incredulously: "You don't mean to say you're Pastor Niemöller?"

"I am Niemöller," said the German. "I can't help it!"

For a moment the sergeant was speechless. Then a rapt expression came over his face as he said ecstatically: "Do you know what I'd like to do? I'd like to kiss you! Hey, fellers!" he said, calling to his men. "Do you know who this is? This man is Pastor Niemöller! Do you know who Niemöller is? You don't! Why, he's a national hero!" And before Niemöller had time to feel embarrassed, the American seized his hand and shook it vigorously in farewell. A minute later the big car swept past and its headlights vanished up the road. The two Germans were alone. One of them had tears in his eyes.

At a quarter to six on the morning of 24 June, 1945, Frau Niemöller was awakened by the sound of a voice calling from under her window. She looked out and saw a man wearing an elegant pepper-and-salt coat of distinctly feminine cut and a slouch hat. All the same, and even if she had not been able to follow her husband's movements from the radio news bulletins, she would have known him anywhere.

Chapter Eight

IN SEARCH OF WORLD PEACE

(1945–7)

THOUGH freedom was sweet Niemöller was not to be allowed to enjoy it in peace. After the happiness of reunion came harsh reality. The cramped conditions and perpetual turmoil in the temporary lodgings in Leoni, where he was struggling amid family, friends and visitors to write some dozens of letters a day in an attempt to pick up the threads of his former existence, made it harder for him to adjust himself to normal life. Everyone seemed nervous and ineffective. Later Frau Niemöller referred to these weeks as the most trying of her whole life.

Worse than these private and basically very understandable difficulties was the realization that Germany itself was becoming one vast concentration camp. The Germans, most of whom were glad to be rid of Hitler's yoke, felt they had been cheated by their liberators. Life after the capitulation failed to come up to their expectations. Admittedly, they no longer had to spend their nights in the air-raid shelter; on the other hand, almost everyone felt he was being treated as a criminal, or at best as a criminal's accomplice. There was a spate of arrests and deportations involving the guilty and the innocent alike. The art of denunciation was flourishing as scarcely ever before in German history. Millions of Germans who had been driven out of the conquered territories in the east made extra mouths to feed. While the occupation troops, who were strictly forbidden all personal contact with the civilian population, were demonstratively setting fire to their surplus food supplies, most Germans were at a loss to feed themselves and their children. One of Niemöller's first official duties after his return was to bury a fifty-year-old woman who had reached Western Germany in the great trek from the east and then died of exhaustion on the day after her arrival, weighing only 3 st. 8 lb.

It was not difficult for an impartial observer to recognize the spiritual dangers implicit in a situation of this kind. Numerous conversations showed Niemöller how deeply nihilism and cynicism had eaten into the souls of his fellow-countrymen. The world in which hitherto they had been living, and compelled to live, with its false and genuine ideals, had collapsed about them; they had been ready to meet the new conditions without prejudice and now, to their boundless disappointment, experience was proving the new to be little better or any more predictable than the old. The immediate consequence was that the Germans' hearts, so recently opened in trust, or at least in favourable expectation, now firmly closed and became hardened. Moreover it was particularly distressing for Niemöller as a churchman to see that, confronted as they were with so much alien guilt, the German people were losing all awareness of their own. Wherever Germans talked among themselves during those years of hunger and despair, the phrase recurred: "After all, the others are no better."

Niemöller was convinced that in this darkness and confusion only the Church was competent to bring clarity and comfort, and naturally, to his mind, the Confessing Church above all others, in view of its record as so effective an opponent of Hitler and the German Christians. But where, in that summer of 1945, was the Confessing Church to be found? Those members who had not died in Hitler's concentration camps and on his battle-fields, or who were not now prisoners in the hands of the Allies, would have to be convened to concert future action. How could they be located in the first instance? The postal services and the railways were still largely disorganized and even short journeys by rail involved endless difficulties for Germans, while interzonal travel required a Military Government permit and that was well-nigh impossible to get. A peace-time trip to Honolulu or Peking was now almost easier to arrange than a journey from Leoni in Bavaria to Hamburg or Berlin, and would certainly be far less eventful. But there was no harm in trying.

A month after his liberation, in July, 1945, Niemöller addressed a memorandum to the Occupying Powers on the situation and prospects of the Evangelical Church, basing his by no means optimistic conclusions on his experiences in the Battle of the Churches against Hitler and later in captivity. He complained particularly of the fact that the leadership of the Churches was still in the hands of those "neutrals" who had shirked taking up an unequivocal attitude under the Hitler régime, and whom he looked on, therefore, as more dangerous even than Hitler's own "German Christians". His conclusion took the form of a demand: "It is all-important, therefore, that the Confessing Church should be given the opportunity which it at present lacks. I am convinced that it is through the Confessing Church that the only possible way can be found, as far as the Evangelical Churches are concerned, to achieve a genuine re-orientation of the spiritual life of our people."

Four weeks later, on 21 August, 1945, the Reich Council of Brethren as the governing body of the Confessing Church was called, held its first post-war meeting in Frankfurt-am-Main. Even Karl Barth managed to attend, arriving from Switzerland without a permit, disguised in a G.I. uniform and driving in a jeep lent him by an American friend. Most of those present were seeing old friends again after many intervening years of suffering, and the reunion was a moving experience. But the meeting did not spend much time in discussing the past. The present situation was considered and a delegation elected to represent the Confessing Church at the forthcoming conference of the German Evangelical Church taking place in the small town of Treysa in Hesse, a conference to which neither Niemöller nor the Confessing Church had originally been invited. Then the meeting considered practical means of giving quick and effective help to the millions of refugees from Eastern Germany.

Finally, the meeting considered a burning contemporary question—the responsibility for the catastrophic events of the previous ten years. It was unanimously agreed that the Churches as well as all Christians in Germany could not disclaim their share of guilt. Niemöller welcomed the spirit which prevailed at this meeting of the Confessing Church, calling it afterwards "the finest demonstration of truly fraternal solidarity in serious and practical discussion ever granted us".

In Treysa, a few days later, a very different atmosphere prevailed. This first post-war meeting of the "official" Church with the Confessing Church provoked serious conflicts of opinion, for the members of the latter considered that they ought to be in the other men's shoes. The wounds of the recent past were still too fresh and it was therefore not surprising that current differences of opinion concerning the Churches' political record during the Hitler period should cast their shadows over the conference at Treysa.

The bitterest disappointment for Niemöller was the gulf which was shown to exist between the Lutherans and the other Protestant confessions. The differences which had dwindled in importance during the fight against Hitler were now coming to the fore again in an alarming manner. Considerable forces within the Churches were more intent on stressing the points in which they differed instead of those on which there was agreement. Already the joint celebration of Holy Communion was being criticized. At the second Synod of the Confessing Church held in Dahlem in 1935 there seemed to have been general agreement that confessional differences between Protestants were of secondary importance only. Now Confessionalism seemed once again to be rampant and threatening to frustrate all efforts to achieve the unification of the Evangelical Church.

During these years Niemöller never tired of calling attention to this danger, at the same time holding up the joint Holy Communion celebrated in Dachau as an example of true Christian fellowship. A few months later, when it became clearer still that some prominent Church leaders had separatist aims, Niemöller bluntly warned his fellow-churchmen against reviving the denominational differences of the sixteenth century, lest in so doing they brought about the schism of the German Evangelical Church. He stated: "The declarations of Faith of the Reformation, above all the Lutheran declarations are quite simply inadequate today to serve as a basis for the unification or for the dismemberment of the Church. . . . Let us hear more of the Word of God, and less about what happened in 1529!"

Niemöller felt that these things needed saying, though he knew well enough that his words would not win him friends among the latter-day Confessionalists.

In Treysa the separatist tendencies had been kept within bounds by the preoccupation with more pressing problems arising out of the prevailing chaos and distress in Germany. A number of men were elected to manage the affairs of the Evangelical Church in Germany and to them the Confessing Church surrendered its claim to the leadership. The first of these was the Bishop of Württemberg, Dr. Wurm, whose name had become famous in the Third Reich in connexion with his courageous stand against euthanasia, practised by the Nazis on the mentally ill. Martin Niemöller was elected as his deputy on the proposal of Professor Karl Barth. Niemöller was also entrusted, by the representatives of the 26 Churches, with the conduct of foreign relations on behalf of the German Protestants, thus becoming their "Foreign Minister". Pleased though he was with these appointments, Niemöller nevertheless left Treysa firmly convinced that an immediate winding-up of the Confessing Church would be premature. In a circular letter sent soon after the conference to his friends, Niemöller wrote: "Far from being over, the usefulness of the Confessing Church is perhaps only now beginning."

In the autumn of 1945 the inevitable reaction after years of anxiety and undernourishment set in, and Niemöller suddenly succumbed to exhaustion and was compelled to rest for a while in a sanatorium in Bavaria. Since his liberation he had been living alternately with his family in Leoni and his sister in Frankfurt, and this unsettled existence, coupled with the lack of regular routine in his work, may have contributed to his break-down. If he could have had his wish, he would have returned to Dahlem. As in the old days in Münster, parish work was what he really longed for, but there was no vacancy for a pastor in Dahlem—that created by his own arrest had long since been filled. "I know," he wrote, "that my duty lies with the Evangelical Church in Germany, though so far no post has been forthcoming in which I can remain even through the coming winter, and although I sorely miss an opening to do some kind of parish work." Frustration allied to physical exhaustion made recovery slow, until some wonderful news instilled new energy into him.

In the middle of October Niemöller received a message from his second son, Hermann, to the effect that he had succeeded in escaping from Czechoslovakia, where he had been held as a prisoner-of-war, and was now in Berlin. In view of the risk involved in travelling from Berlin to the Western Zones for any young German of military age, Niemöller decided he would fetch his son from Berlin himself. Thanks to the Americans, who, among other assistance, lent him a U.S. army car, Niemöller succeeded in bringing his son out of Berlin and out of the Russian Zone without papers of any kind.

While in Berlin, Niemöller visited his old parish of Dahlem. It was a depressing experience. The rectory where he and his family had lived was partially destroyed and the contents had been looted. The once wealthy parish had been reduced to extreme poverty. Most of the inhabitants were living—or trying to stay alive—on the lowest category of ration card, No. 5, known to Berliners as the "death card" because its entitlement of 1000 calories per day gave its adult owner the certainty of slowly starving to death. Despite unimaginable privations, however, the inhabitants of Dahlem, and other Berlin parishes where conditions were no better, had made a habit of laying aside the first slice from every loaf of bread for the refugees from the east. In the mornings girls went from door to door collecting the slices and then took them to the railway stations, transit camps and cross-roads and distributed them to the starving people as they arrived en route for the west. Though Christ-like, this was not Christian charity in the sense that it had been organized by the Church. No theologian stood sponsor to this act of compassion, nor had it been on the agenda at any ecclesiastical conference. Human nature does not always need to be preached at in order to act sublimely. There was a lesson in all this for Niemöller, as there was in the dreadful sight of truck upon truckload of starved, skeletal humanity that arrived daily, hourly almost, at the railway terminus from Eastern Germany. Whose fault was this? Who was responsible? How did it come about and what could Germans do to make sure it never happened again?

It was the Russians' fault, many Berliners would say. They were the guilty ones — they and their yes-men, the Americans and the British. Goebbels had been right: to fight Russia was to fight barbarism. The flower of German youth had been sacrificed in defence of European civilization, but instead of helping to roll back the Red tide, the British and Americans had brought it to the very heart of Europe. They would live to regret it. Now Germans were suffering; soon it would be the Allies' turn.

Niemöller saw how his countrymen, in their bitterness and prejudice, had eyes only for other nations' guilt. How, he wondered, could it be made easier for them to recognize their own? For he was more than ever convinced that, unless they did so, there could be no spiritual rebirth in Germany and all the millions who were now suffering would have suffered in vain. The past would serve merely as a precedent instead of as a warning for the future. Germans must recognize their own sins of omission and commission, must have the humility to admit them, and the desire to learn from them for their own and their children's sakes. A beginning could be made, felt Niemöller, in this process of self-examination if a lead were given by the Churches. He awaited his opportunity.

The opportunity came when Niemöller went to Stuttgart to attend the first meeting of the newly-formed Council of the Evangelical Church. On the way to Stuttgart from Leoni, Niemöller discovered from a short paragraph in a small local newspaper that he was expected to preach the sermon that same evening at a service to be held in the largest surviving church in Stuttgart. Bishop Wurm and Bishop Dibelius were also to preach, before a congregation which was to include some of the leading foreign Protestant churchmen. Niemöller had time only to choose the text for his sermon. Arriving in Stuttgart, he went straight from the car into the church.

The text was from Jeremiah, chapter 14, verses 17–22:

"Therefore thou shalt say this word unto them; Let mine eyes run down with tears night and day, and let them not cease; for the virgin daughter of my people is broken with a great breach, with a very grievous blow.

"If I go forth into the field, then behold the slain with the sword! and if I enter into the city, then behold them that are sick with famine! yea, both the prophet and the priest go about into a land that they know not.

"Hast thou utterly rejected Judah? hath thy soul loathed Zion? why has thou smitten us, and there is no healing for us? we looked for peace, and there is no good; and for the time of healing, and behold trouble!

"We acknowledge, O Lord, our wickedness, and the iniquity of our fathers: for we have sinned against thee.

"Do not abhor us, for thy name's sake, do not disgrace the throne of thy glory: remember, break not thy covenant with us.

"Are there any among the vanities of the Gentiles that can cause rain? or can the heavens give showers? art not thou he, O Lord our God? therefore we will wait upon thee: for thou hast made all these things."

As Niemöller read these words from the pulpit, many of the congregation were struck by their extraordinary relevance to the current situation in Germany. They were to provide the *leit-motif* of the discussions on the following day, which began on the subject of the relations between the German Evangelical Church and foreign Churches. Before starting with the agenda proper, the Germans had agreed that they should make it clear to their guests of the Ecumenical Council that they fully recognized their own share of responsibility for the terrible events of the previous twelve years. This was the essential basis for any sincere and fruitful co-operation with world Christendom. So the newly elected delegates of the Evangelical Church drew up that declaration that has since found a place in history as "the Stuttgart Declaration of Guilt". Its contents were communicated to the delegates which the Geneva World Council of Churches had sent to Stuttgart in a special session on that same day.

We find it difficult, when reading the text of this declaration today, to understand why it provoked such an immense outcry among wide sections of the German public. After speaking of the great fellowship of suffering, but also of the solidarity of guilt which the Church shared with the German people, the following key sentences occur in the Declaration:

> "We say with great sorrow: through us endless suffering has been brought to many peoples and lands. That which we have often testified before our parishes we now proclaim in the name of the whole Church: though we fought in the name of Jesus Christ for long years against the spirit which found terrible expression in the National Socialist terror-régime, we accuse ourselves of not having borne witness more courageously, not having prayed more faithfully, believed more joyously and loved with greater ardour. Now a new beginning is to be made in our Churches. . . ."

That was honest, sober, clear and unequivocal. It did not fail to make its effect on the representatives of foreign Churches. The Frenchman, Pierre Maury, spoke for all when he said: "It cannot have been easy for you to speak in such terms. Only in Jesus Christ can your hearts have been opened to do so. We understand that you wish to keep faith with your own people. We can only be grateful for that. You thought, wrote and proclaimed that message before God. Through Grace it is acceptable to God. It is *our* task not to stand before you with pharisaical pride."

Foreigners had understood that which many Germans could not or would not understand, though in fairness it must be granted that it was not always made easy for them to understand aright. This was the time when propagandists of hate and revenge launched the conception of the Germans' "collective guilt" on the world, in order thereby to strike at the German people as a whole. Such individuals were only too ready to misuse the Stuttgart Declaration for their own propagandistic ends, knowingly misinterpreting it although they were well aware that it had nothing to do with day-to-day politics. Similarly, the newspapers and radio stations controlled by the Occupying Powers put out tendentious reports of what had happened at Stuttgart, despite the repeated assertions of Niemöller and other Evangelical spokesmen that they entirely rejected the political conception of a collective guilt. "Without a collective conscience there can be no such thing as collective guilt," stated Niemöller when speaking to National Socialists interned in the fortress of Hohen-Asperg. "This is, rather, a question of the individual's guilt, and the individual's responsibility."

For Niemöller the Declaration of Stuttgart was, and is, the salient event in the life of the German people and of the Evangelical Church since the end of the war. Despite misunderstandings and abuse, he maintains his adherence to it. "Yes, I was one of those who subscribed to the Declaration of Guilt. We could do no else, although we knew we would be called traitors." When students in Erlangen, Göttingen and Marburg noisily protested, Niemöller remained unmoved. Yet he spoke for those same students when Military Government and the university authorities threatened them with punishment. He could well sympathize with the young Germans of 1945, he wrote in a letter to the Rector of Erlangen, and went on to speak of his own similar feelings after the First World War. "When a preacher at a service in the Church of Zion in Bethel told us that we Christians in Germany bore our own full measure of responsibility for the war and its outcome—and that at a time when the Versailles Treaty had just been signed—I could not help it, I had to leave." The *Neue Zeitung*, a newspaper published and financed by the Americans, had no sympathy with such an attitude. "It is neither legitimate nor desirable for a newspaper to indulge in charity of this kind," stated an editorial, and went on to urge that the students should be punished.

After the paralysing lethargy of the previous months, Niemöller now thought to see a new beginning for the Christian message. During the next few years he was to attempt to explain from pulpit and platform to Evangelical Christians in all four Occupation Zones what the Stuttgart Declaration was, and was not, intended to convey. He called on the people to show a sense of responsibility towards their fellow-men, he abjured them not to forget the lessons of the past and, above all, he reminded them constantly of the burden of guilt which had to be redeemed before a new life could begin. In so doing he was at pains not to exclude himself from a like responsibility, and told in this connexion the story of the visit which he and his wife paid to Dachau in the autumn of 1945. After showing her the cell in which he had been confined for so many months, they passed the crematorium. A great white-painted board had been affixed to a tree and on it, in black letters, they read:

"Here between the years 1933 and 1945 238,756 human beings were incinerated."

At that moment, Niemöller told his audience, the consciousness of his own guilt and his own failure assailed him as never before. "And God asked me—as once He asked the First Man

Pastor Niemöller preaching in Basle, 1946

after the Fall, Adam—Man, where wast thou in those years
1933 to 1945? I knew I had no answer to that question. True, I
had an alibi in my pocket, for the years 1937 to 1945, my identity disc from the concentration camp. But what help to me was
that? God was not asking me where I had been from 1937 to
1945, but from 1933 to 1945, and for the years 1933 to 1937 I
had no answer. Should I have said perhaps: 'As a pastor in
those years I bore courageous witness to the Faith; I dared to
speak, and risked life and freedom in doing so?' But God did
not ask about that. God asked: 'Where were you from 1933 to
1945 when human beings were incinerated here? . . . When, in
1933, Goering publicly boasted that all active Communists had
been imprisoned and rendered harmless—that was when we
forgot our responsibility, that was when we should have warned
our parishioners. Many a man from my own parish, who went
and joined the National Socialist Party and who is now to do
penance for his act, could rise up against me today and say that
he would have acted differently if I had not kept silence at that
time. . . . I know that I made my contribution towards the en-
slavement of the German people. . . ."

Niemöller was going about the land like a modern Jeremiah,
wrote the Swiss newspaper, *Semeur Vaudois*, referring to his
penitential homilies. "The similarity between the two men is
staggering. Is Niemöller, too, destined to die spurned and un-
comprehended by the people whom he tried to save?" A terrible
question, particularly in the light of Niemöller's own summing-
up, which he made several years later in a speech to former
prisoners-of-war: "For two years I have done nothing else but
preach this Declaration of Guilt—unfortunately without success. Material distress has now largely been abolished, at least
in the western half of Germany, but spiritual rigor is far advanced. The opportunity of Stuttgart has been missed."

All the greater was the echo which the Declaration of Stuttgart found in world Christendom, both on the material and the
spiritual plane. Most of the gifts sent to Germany during the

period when privations were at their worst came from Christians who, in many cases, made some personal sacrifice in sending them. A further direct consequence of the Declaration of Guilt was the invitation extended to the Germans to take part in the work of the Ecumenical Council. Niemöller was asked to sit on the Provisional Committee of the recently formed World Council of Churches. In February, 1946, he made his first visit to Geneva to take part in the first large Ecumenical gathering since the end of the war. He was touched by the warmth of the welcome extended to him, the representative of a nation that had so recently fought under a pagan banner. Bishop Berggrav, for example, who had led the clerical resistance to Hitler in Norway and who was said to have appeared for a discussion at the Berlin Foreign Office, before the war had actually begun, pointedly holding a photograph of Niemöller in his hand, now welcomed him with outstretched arms. Kissing Niemöller, he said with emotion: "Dear brother Niemöller, I have been looking forward to this moment for so many months!" The Bishop of Denmark also, where the Church had similarly suffered under the German occupation, refrained in his report from laying the chief stress on that period with its bitter memories, and praised instead the "Confessing Church" of Germany to which Danish Protestantism owed in no small measure its own survival of war and persecution. Not only at this meeting, but on many occasions later, proof was forthcoming of the respect in which Niemöller was held by Christians throughout the world, on account of his resistance to Hitler. The General Secretary of the World Council of Churches, Dr. W. A. Visser't Hooft, gave expression to it in connexion with Neimöller's sixtieth birthday in 1952 when he said: "Countless people all over the world are glad that we have a Martin Niemöller among us."

Meanwhile, Niemöller's private life was fraught with many problems. The parish for which he yearned was still not forthcoming and he still lacked a permanent home where he could work in peace and live with his family. Staying in strongly

Lutheran Bavaria also had its complications. Niemöller's sermons, with their passionate advocacy of a *rapprochement* between German Protestant Denominations, had not gained him any friends among rigid Confessionalists, who were particularly numerous in Bavaria, and it eventually came to the point when no clergy in the province would lend him a pulpit.

A visit which the provincial Bishop, Dr. Meiser, then paid him in Leoni in an attempt to come to some arrangement ended in failure despite goodwill and the desire for reconciliation on both sides. Their conversation ended with a statement by the Lutheran Bishop to the effect that he felt a closer affinity to the Roman Catholics than to his fellow-Protestants of the reformed let alone of the United Church.

In the midst of this unfortunate situation an old acquaintance, Fürst von Isenburg-Büdingen, invited Niemöller and his family to stay with him at his castle in Hessen. Niemöller had officiated at his host's wedding in 1936 and when the latter was imprisoned after the war as a former member of the Nazi Party, Niemöller had successfully appealed for his release. Niemöller gladly accepted the invitation; it meant food and shelter for his family for the coming winter, and the necessary space for himself in which to continue the work, already begun in Leoni, of establishing contact with the Churches in other countries and developing relations with them.

Niemöller and his family moved to Büdingen in December, 1945. They were to remain there until May, 1948. The medieval castle with its towers and massive walls of stone formed the romantic setting for a most unromantic, prosaic but purposeful labour in the cause of the Churches' reconstruction. Much as they all welcomed it, the move entailed a somewhat difficult upheaval for the Niemöller family. As most of their possessions had been destroyed or stolen during the siege of Berlin, all they could take with them to Büdingen were a few beds and cupboards.

To start with, Niemöller's main task consisted in recruiting suitable staff for the different departments of the Ecclesiastical "Foreign Office". He obtained the services of Pastors Koller and Bartelt from Württemberg and Pomerania, as office supervisor he engaged an ex-Admiral, Johannesson by name, and he made his old friend, the ex-General of Infantry Dr. Franz Beyer, his private secretary, having first had to expedite his release from an internment camp. The group was completed later by the addition of the Westphalian pastor, Gerhard Stratenwerth, who together with Niemöller had been appointed assistant to the first "Reich Bishop", Friedrich von Bodelschwingh, in the spring of 1933. He now became Niemöller's deputy.

While at Büdingen Niemöller paid his first visits to foreign countries. During the course of the years they were to take him to all parts of the earth and to many countries of the "eastern" as well as of the "western" world, earning him increasing right to the title once given him by the Bishop of Berlin, Dr. Dibelius, of "Ambassador Extraordinary of the German People". One of the most important of these journeys was a six-month lecture tour in the United States which Niemöller, accompanied by his wife, undertook in the winter of 1946 at the invitation of the Federal Council of the Churches of Christ. It was the first time a well-known figure from conquered Germany had been given such an opportunity. Niemöller lectured to over two hundred audiences, of which forty were clerical and seventeen consisted of university students.

He experienced and aroused much goodwill which was to find expression in the coming years in the form of practical assistance to starving Germany. In the western states where, hitherto, public attention had been concentrated largely on the Far East, he succeeded in stimulating interest in the problems affecting Europe. During his American lecture tour Niemöller developed a characteristically evangelizing style which was to be his most effective defence against political and personal attacks. The style was essentially that of a religious preacher who, however topical his theme, never allowed the discussion of current problems to obscure the fact that he was first and foremost a churchman delivering a Christian message.

During the course of this tour Niemöller became a highly controversial figure. Some of the attacks made on him were remarkably similar in tone to those of the Hitler period. The call to penance and reconciliation which he sounded was out of harmony with the theme of vengeance and reprisal which dominated public opinion on the eve of the Moscow Conference. One of Niemöller's most prominent and forceful opponents was President Roosevelt's widow, Mrs. Eleanor Roosevelt. While paying due tribute to Niemöller's record during the Nazi régime, she maintained that a former U-boat commander who, she claimed, was well known for his nationalist opinions, was not the right man to speak for the new, post-war Germany in the United States. The publicist Victor Bernstein made a yet stronger attack in the New York left-wing newspaper, *PM*, stating: "Europe's dead will not be avenged by men who volunteered to go to war for Hitler in 1939." The Rabbi, Abba Hillel Silver, from Cleveland, maintained that Niemöller had never opposed the National Socialist racial theories, but merely the suppression of the Church in Germany. Another Rabbi, Stephen S. Wise from New York contested Niemöller's assertion that anti-Semitism in Germany was dead. The columnist, John P. Lewis seconded him with the words: "Pastor Niemöller has come to America to tell us that anti-Semitism in Germany is dead. If the pastor looked a little more closely he would see that it is the Jews who have died."

Though such reactions to Niemöller's first visit to America cannot be passed over in silence, it would be wrong to look on them as typical and thereby lend them more importance than they deserve—they should be seen, rather, against the contemporary background of bitterness and recrimination. Discordant notes were struck on Niemöller's numerous later visits to America, also, but they were insignificant compared with the chorus of approval which his listeners and fellow Christians sounded wherever he went, and above all, with the tangible effects of his mission.

In Holland, two years later, Niemöller achieved an outstanding success in winning the hearts of 8000 young Dutchmen at the World Conference of Churches. This was not only a triumph for the cause to which he had devoted all his energies for the last twenty years, but it was also a most valuable link of fellowship with a nation that had suffered particularly at the hands of Germany and the Germans.

The mission which Niemöller, accompanied by his wife, undertook in 1949 in Australia at the invitation of a small interconfessional organization known as "The Open Air Campaigners", also served the double purpose of an evangelizing tour and a goodwill visit. Before reaching Australia, the plane made an intermediate landing in Honolulu. Garlanded with flowers, Niemöller preached to the Christians on the island of Oahu, and the grim description he gave of conditions in Germany contrasted strangely with the warm tropical night filled with the gentle rustle of the palms under the pulsing, starlit sky. The reception accorded him in Australia was no less cordial than in the United States, and it gave him particular pleasure to accept the hospitality which the Lutherans pressed on him wherever he went, although the Lutheran Church did not take part in the work of the Open Air Campaigners. Almost in every Lutheran parish Niemöller visited, he and his wife were guests at the vicarage and in reporting later on his travels he laid particular stress on this fact. The success of the visit to Australia was such that Dr. Mowll, the Archbishop of Sydney and head of the Anglican Church in Australia, described Niemöller in one of his addresses as "the most outstanding personality in the history of the Christian Church since Martin Luther".

Amongst the numerous duties awaiting Niemöller as head of the Ecclesiastical "Foreign Office" in the summer of 1947, after his return from America, was that of attending the World Conference of Christian Youth in Oslo. In other respects also, the

Niemöller greeting those taking part in the "Procession of Witness" in Sydney on September 10, 1949 second half of the year 1947 was to be important. On 1 October the constituent Synod of the Evangelical Church of Hessen and Nassau, which represented an amalgamation of the three previously independent Churches of Hessen, Nassau and Frankfurt-am-Main, adopted by 84 votes to 27 a resolution proposing Niemöller as first President of the Church and framed in the following terms:

"The Synod considers it of primary importance that relations should be established and maintained in the person of the President both with the Evangelical Church in Germany and with the Ecumenical Council and in recognition of his work in both these connexions the Synod elects Pastor Martin Niemöller to the Presidency of the Evangelical Church in Hessen and Nassau."

Niemöller accepted the appointment on the condition that he should be allowed to continue his work as "Foreign Minister" of the German Evangelical Church. His official residence as Church President of Hessen and Nassau was Wiesbaden to start with, the world-famed spa and former seat of the Dukes of Nassau. Thither Niemöller and his family moved in May, 1948. Some years later the Synod decided to transfer the President's headquarters to Darmstadt, the former capital of the Grand Duchy of Hessen. At the same time the work of the "Foreign Office" had outgrown the accommodation at Büdingen and the staff moved to Frankfurt.

Church President of Hessen-Nassau! At last the wish which Niemöller had cherished since his return from the concentration camp had come true: he was once more in close contact with the Church's day-to-day parish work. From now on he would be using the knowledge and experience gained through his work in Germany for the benefit of the German-speaking communities abroad, whose welfare was not the least of his responsibilities as "Foreign Minister", and vice versa. The two appointments which he now held were thus complementary—a fact overlooked by critics who complained that the Church President spent too much of his time abroad.

In accepting his new office, Niemöller, true to his life-long Protestant convictions, had resolutely opposed the suggested title of "Bishop". In his opinion, the office of bishop was a non-Evangelical conception and he also preferred the designation of "Church President" on the grounds that it would be less liable to be misconstrued by his fellow-clergy. For the same reasons he declined to allow the dignitaries of his church to wear gold crosses or any other outward symbols of their high office. In expressing these views to the Synod of the Hessen-Nassau Church Niemöller further based them on the desire to show some tangible proof of penance in regard to the events of the recent past, and in due course the Synod adopted his proposals by the large majority of 116 votes to 20.

One of the most important of the regulations of the new Hessen-Nassau Church was the following: "The Church President shall be ruled by the decisions of the Church Synod and shall be answerable to the Church Synod in the performance of his office." Niemöller had already learned, when he was Manager of the Home Mission for Westphalia and during his early days as Pastor in Dahlem, that in a healthy Evangelical Church the "centre of gravity" lies with the parishes, and the situation envisaged by this regulation was therefore one which he knew and approved. During the following years he considered it one of his main tasks as Church President to strengthen the parishes, rather than to increase the power and authority of the Church as such. Security, power, respect—to achieve these had always at all times been a strong temptation to churchmen, he knew, and Niemöller was not afraid to admit that the temptation still existed. "We leaders of the Church are perpetually in danger of leading it astray by concentrating our efforts on establishing it in its power, whereas only the Church itself, in other words, the rank and file in the parishes, can ensure that the leaders themselves do not become godless."

A favourite and most effective way of assuring the Church's position, but also a most dangerous one, had been for centuries past to seek the protection of the State. This Niemöller knew well enough from his own experiences under the Hitler régime and he was therefore particularly concerned to see the Church condone by its silence certain policies carried out by the Occupying Powers with the co-operation of the newly created Land governments, thereby threatening to forfeit the respect and confidence of the German people. Was the Church in agreement, for example, with the unjust and over-systematized procedure of de-Nazification, which all too frequently penalized the small fry while allowing the outstanding offenders to escape? Why did not the Church protest? How could these huge-scale reprisals be reconciled with the Sermon on the Mount, with the Beatitudes and with the teaching of Seventy-Times-Seven? It was not easy to answer these questions justly and dispassionately, particularly as those who posed them frequently had ulterior motives for doing so. Niemöller knew well that de-Nazification was, in principle, sound and very necessary. But in practice it had long since become a farce and, worse still, grossly unjust in innumerable cases. It would be both callous and irresponsible, Niemöller considered, to keep silence any longer. One Sunday in February, 1948, a statement signed by himself was read from every Evangelical pulpit within the area of authority of the Hessen-Nassau Church. It attacked the methods of de-Nazification and forbade the clergy and their parishioners to co-operate further with the arbitration tribunals. In its blunt wording the declaration was reminiscent of many of Niemöller's sermons during the Battle of the Churches in which he attacked the Nazi attempts to introduce racial discrimination into the Church. And the content of the declaration also referred directly to that period, when it called de-Nazification an instrument of reprisal reviving the terrors of the Hitler régime. "People in their hundreds of thousands are giving way to constant pressure to tell lies. The old system of placing an offender's entire family under arrest has returned. Tens of thousands of people have lost their employment and the means of earning their living, while they await in internment either their sentence or, long after its announcement, the day when they will be released."

Although the Stuttgart Declaration of Guilt should have been sufficient guarantee that Niemöller's statement would not be misconstrued, wide sections of so-called public opinion in fact greeted it with a storm of indignation. In terms all too redolent of the Third Reich the government of Hessen, Military Government and left-wing politicians accused him of "unauthorized interference in matters of State". The Berlin *Tagesspiegel*, a recently founded newspaper appearing under American licence, published an indignant article by a retired State official in which the writer lamented the fact that "the Christian mantle of love should be held perpetually in readiness to cloak and condone an act of civil disobedience". This "pastoral letter", continued the article, showed Niemöller once again as "a problematical character who, despite his spiritual office, does not use his influence to achieve peace and reconciliation, but on the contrary acts as an aggressive and disturbing element". Besides many conversations with individuals of all shades of political opinion, Niemöller's personal mail showed him, however, that his declaration reflected the general public feeling regarding de-Nazification. It was a source of some satisfaction to him that, soon after, the Catholic bishops made a similar, though more moderate protest. When the Social Democrats in Frankfurt attempted to prevent him speaking at the re-dedication ceremony of the famous Church of St. Paul*, Niemöller was not deterred and succeeded in delivering his address without any public disturbance taking place.

The task of fusing three Churches with differing traditions presented Church President Niemöller with a wide variety of

---

* Church of St. Paul in Frankfurt-am-Main. Protestant Church in the centre of the city. It was here in the years 1848/9 that the bourgeois liberals made their unsuccessful attempt to establish Germany as a Kaiserreich on the occasion of the first German National Assembly. The church was destroyed by American bombs in the Second World War and was rebuilt in 1949. It is used today as a conference and exhibition hall.

problems. An ecclesiastical code had to be drawn up which would satisfy each of the three that its own interests were not being sacrificed, or those of the others preferred, and an attempt had to be made to harmonize Church Law as quickly as possible in each of the three areas. Large numbers of refugees from Eastern Germany, who were used to a totally different Church organization, had to be assimilated and made to feel at home. Thousands of parcels of food, clothing and medical supplies were sent from the parishes in Hessen-Nassau to the Church of Saxony, in the other half of Germany, which this West German church had undertaken to "adopt". From the beginning Niemöller strove to achieve the best possible relations with the Roman Catholic Church. During his first few years as President he arranged regular meetings with the Catholic bishops of Mainz and Limburg, both of which towns were in his Church's area. Catholic refugees who were directed to settle in areas with a Protestant population were welcomed as guests in Evangelical churches. As the connecting link between all these tasks, stood the motto—"strengthening of the parishes".

In the days of the Battle of the Churches, even Niemöller's friends had declared it impossible to imagine him as a Church dignitary. Now he was visibly growing in stature as he mastered the new role of Church President and it gave him great satisfaction to observe how, under his guidance, the interdenominational differences between members of the United, Reformed and Lutheran Churches were beginning to receive no more than fitting recognition as had been the case during the Battle of the Churches, and at the time of the Declaration of Barmen.

Since the Treysa Conference in the autumn of 1945, the development of the German Evangelical Church, of which the Hessen-Nassau Church formed a part, had followed a very different course. The thirteen Lutheran Churches who came under its aegis were almost solidly in favour of forming a new organization, "The United Evangelical Lutheran Churches of Germany", and had no intention of sacrificing any of their confessional characteristics in the interests of the national body. As a result, the Evangelical Church had degenerated into a loose association of autonomous Churches, most of them aggressively defending their own peculiarities. The painful fact was becoming increasingly clear that German Protestantism consisted of two antagonistic groups: on the one hand, the thirteen Lutheran Churches comprising a population of approximately seventeen millions, and on the other, the two Reformed and eleven United Churches with about the same number of adherents. Moreover the Church Conference at Eisenach in July, 1948, and the Bethel Synod of January, 1949, showed that the "Confessing Church" was no longer powerful enough to offer a common platform to the separatist portions of the Evangelical Church, a function which it had so effectively performed in the early stages of the Hitler period—"a state of affairs to make one weep" wrote Niemöller in a letter to his brother. Admittedly, agreement was reached on a "basic order" for the Evangelical Church, but this was because neither the Lutherans nor the other Churches wanted to bring about a final split, and no one was deceived into thinking that the new regulations were anything but purely organizational. In the words of the late Bishop Wurm, the new Evangelical Church of Germany was merely a "temporary hutment", and Niemöller confirmed that it was "not an impressive edifice", much to his regret, for hitherto he had continued to hope that events might take a different course. "Much will depend in future," he wrote, "on whether the two main points of view prove compatible in practice, and on whether those who hold them show mutual tolerance."

Despite these serious and persistent differences within the Evangelical Church there was at least one problem on which— as the Conference of Eisenach showed—the Lutherans and the members of the Reformed and United Churches were agreed. Both groups clearly realized that, for the sake of humanity for which they—as in the Hitler period—felt themselves jointly responsible, the third world war which the politicians were discussing must be prevented at all costs. They agreed in condemning all types of crusading political ideologies and the methods of the "cold war" which, if not countered soon enough, would ultimately lead to bloodshed. The document entitled "A Word to the Parishes" which was framed, largely by Niemöller, at the Eisenach Conference gave clear expression to this conviction in warning Evangelical Christians not to allow themselves to become the instruments of a propaganda that aimed at spreading enmity between the nations. "In particular we implore all sections of our people not to be deluded into thinking that a new war could bring relief to our communal state of want. . . . No blessing rests on force, and wars lead only to deeper bitterness, hatred, misery and destitution. The world needs love, not force. It needs peace, not war."

The Synod of Bethel underlined this warning by stating that the creation of just social conditions was the best guarantee of peace. In so doing, it revived a warning issued in 1947 by the Council of Brethren of the "Confessing Church", the body of leading churchmen that had re-elected Niemöller as their chairman in 1945. The Council bluntly reproached the Evangelical Church with having neglected its duty in the social sphere: "We rejected the right to rebel, at the same time tolerating and approving the growth of absolute dictatorship. We erred in believing it to be our duty to enter politics and employ political methods in order to form a front of the good people against the bad, of Light against Darkness and of the Just against the Unjust. By taking sides in the formation of political, social and ideological fronts we have set at naught the free offer of God's Grace to all and abandoned the world to self-justification. . . . We erred in overlooking the fact that the economic doctrines of Marxism should have reminded us of our duties towards our flock in regard to their social needs in this world. We have failed to make the cause of the poor and the outcasts the concern of Christians, according to the gospel of the coming Kingdom of God. . . ."

These certainly were hard and unpopular words, words which would sound shrilly in the ears of many a clerical Christian because they struck at the roots of his complacency, but words, nevertheless, which needed saying if the attempt was to be repeated, despite all previous failures, to regulate national and international society according to the commandment of the Sermon on the Mount. The statement was, soon after, completed by a further declaration by the Council of Brethren on the question of Jewish refugees, and by a call for the formation of Evangelical building clubs. Niemöller was one of the driving forces behind all these activities.

A close examination of Niemöller's actions and speeches at that time reveals a new note. Since 1945 his thoughts had been devoted almost exclusively to the problem, "What is to become of the Church?" But now they appeared to turn outwards to consider the problems of humanity for whose weal or woe the Church shared some of the responsibility, or at least, in Niemöller's opinion, ought to feel itself jointly responsible. At first hesitantly and then with increasing assurance he entered the field of politics—not, indeed, as a politician or supporter of any particular party, least of all as a spokesman for any of those groups of interests which, as the political consolidation of Western Germany progressed, were becoming increasingly vocal and purposeful in their activities, but rather as a churchman and Evangelical Christian whose authority derived from no human or earthly power. The process, alike mysterious and logically necessary when considered in relation to the political and spiritual developments of the time, might almost be compared with that inner enlightenment which Niemöller experienced sixteen years before, in 1933. Whereas at that time it was Hitler's attempt to introduce the racial laws into the Church which opened Niemöller's eyes, now it was the fate of the seventeen million Germans living in the Russian Zone which roused him to action. "Before God and men we have no right to abandon these seventeen million people"—that was the burden of the message he delivered in speeches and sermons, making it readily understandable to his audiences by quoting the New Testament parable of the Good Samaritan. Germans in East and West were jointly responsible for the present position, he said. Neither could therefore stand aside while the other bore all the burdens, even though the sharing of them entailed sacrifices. In this connexion Niemöller quoted a West German industrialist friend who had said to him fearfully: "What! You want to take away the Iron Curtain? But don't you realize we would all be bankrupt then?" On a visit to his old parish of Dahlem, Niemöller retorted: "The seventeen million people in the Eastern Zone have no neighbours in the world apart from us in Western Germany!" This was the signal for uproar, but raising his voice above the clamour, Niemöller continued: "It is a matter of indifference to the nations in the East whether these seventeen millions live or die. France would sleep more peacefully if these seventeen millions were dead. The British and the Americans recognize no neighbours apart from one another."

When the West German State received solid foundations in 1949 Niemöller's fear was that the two halves of Germany would from then on become even more rapidly estranged. He foresaw the creation of a similar political structure in the East, which would then compete with the Western State, and he missed no opportunity of warning against this development, which he considered would prove fatal to the ultimate goal of a reunited Germany. When the first elections to the Bonn Assembly were held in August, 1949, Niemöller was being only logical when he refused to vote. When his colleagues returned from recording theirs, he reproached them with: "You have voted today for the division of Germany!"

Shortly afterwards, when Niemöller left for Australia, he was glad to find that events in Germany were more easily seen in perspective from another continent, and he welcomed the chance to realize what many Europeans and also Germans were inclined to forget: Europe and Germany were not the hub of the world; there were other continents and other nations with quite different but no less important problems awaiting solution. When Niemöller returned to Germany in November, he found little change in the political situation, and so was unprepared for the storm which was to break about his ears.

It began with an interview which he gave at 10 p.m. on 11 December in his home in Wiesbaden to a woman reporter of the *New York Herald Tribune*. His diary merely notes for that day: "Visit of an American woman journalist." Miss Margaret Higgins, whom Niemöller had met fleetingly on his American lecture tour, had just come from Korea. She had broken her journey home to call on the German pastor in Wiesbaden to ask him, for the benefit of his many friends and supporters in the U.S.A., for his opinion on current developments in Germany. In a talk lasting an hour and a half, Niemöller answered her questions with complete frankness, after first specifically asking that his statements should not be published in the Press in the form of an interview.

Two days later an extract from the conversation was published in the American and European editions of the *New York Herald Tribune*, and, as with so many interviews, although the statements attributed to Niemöller were correct, the fact that they were condensed and taken out of their context tended to distort their meaning. As a man of impulsive temperament who does not always weigh his every word, Niemöller has often had trouble with the Press on these very grounds, particularly in the politically acrimonious period since 1945. On this occasion, however, the impression conveyed by the Press report was more than usually unfortunate. "Niemöller for United Reich even if it's Red" ran the banner headline. What had Niemöller, in fact, said or intended to convey? He had been asked what the Germans' reaction would be to another war. This was a highly topical question in view of the war in Korea and one which weighed on the minds of many Germans at that time. In reply, Niemöller gave it as his opinion that the majority of his fellow countrymen would accept a foreign dictatorship if by that means both the permanent division of their country and, above all, a bloody war in which German would be fighting against German could be prevented. The solution to the German problem which he personally preferred, was quite a different one, however. The American, Russian, British and French occupation forces should be withdrawn, he suggested, and in their stead United Nations' forces—"a few thousand Swedes, for example"—should take over the administration of a reunited Germany, as contemplated in the Potsdam Agreement. . . . Niemöller claimed that the German people would welcome such an arrangement as paving the way for a single government for all Germany. He suggested that, to start with, its members should be drawn from the existing civil authorities in all Zones.

Those politicians and newspapers whose "conceptions" were at variance with Niemöller's opinions, immediately branded his proposal as unrealistic, childish, naïve and fantastic. But it was not the only source of offence in the interview. A far worse crime in the eyes of his critics was that Niemöller had dared to flout one of the strongest taboos of the newly founded West German State—the conspiracy of silence which prevailed in regard to the confessional situation associated with it. Since the Reformation, Niemöller explained to the American journalist, Protestantism had never suffered such heavy losses in adherents as those brought about by the amputation of Eastern Germany; and he mentioned a fact barely known to the rest of the world, namely that 47 per cent of all Evangelical Germans were now living behind the Iron Curtain as compared with 10 per cent of the former Catholic population of the Reich. Miss Higgins then asked Niemöller's opinion as to who was interested in perpetuating this state of affairs. He did not reply directly, but conveyed his meaning clearly enough when he said that the West German Federal Republic was a structure "begotten in Rome and born in Washington".

The Vatican alleged to be hand in hand with the United States as creators and exploiters of the division of Germany! The publication of this charge provoked a sensation. The reaction was similar to that in 1948 when Niemöller had expressed his views on de-Nazification. Of the 150 letters which reached him daily, the majority thanked the Church President for having had the courage to express openly what the writers themselves had for long been secretly thinking.

All the sharper were the reproofs forthcoming from West German politicians and that portion of the Press which supported them. President Heuss had, no doubt, Niemöller in mind when he spoke in his New Year's address of "a Confessionalism clothed with statistics and mistrust". The Federal Chancellor, Dr. Adenauer, took exception to the phrase "begotten in Rome" as tending to disturb the religious peace.* The same reproach was also forthcoming from Dr. Haug, Dr. Wurm's successor as Bishop of Württemberg, who called Niemöller's statement "far removed from reality". The ex-U-boat Commander had "pressed the wrong button, releasing instead of the periscope a torpedo which had then struck his own fleet".

Once again, as four years previously after the Stuttgart Declaration of Guilt, Niemöller had to expend much time and energy in transforming the shock which he had caused public opinion into a more positive and fruitful stimulus. Though he stated that he would not have used the expression "begotten in Rome and born in Washington" in a public speech and that he did so only in conversation with the American journalist on the understanding that it would not be published, he did not retract it. "Are we no longer allowed to mention facts?" he asked his friend, Dr. Gustav Heinemann, the Bonn Minister of the Interior, in a letter. "Without truth there can be no peace, and that applies equally to peace between the Confessions."

Before long, Niemöller had the satisfaction of seeing well-

* Niemöller's opinion of Dr. Adenauer's Party, the Christian Democratic Union, emerges from a Press item of 10 June, 1950, according to which Niemöller had told a journalist friend that in his opinion the C.D.U. was neither Christian nor democratic.

known Protestants coming to his support. Even the then Professor of Theology at Tübingen University, Helmut Thielicke, for example, who by no means invariably agreed with Niemöller, said cautiously that he had "no doubt correctly observed certain tendencies", and went on to speak of "a Catholic Confessionalization in the Federal Republic". Dr. Hermann Ehlers, who was later to become President of the Federal Assembly and was at that time a member of the High-Consistory in Odlenburg, also gave Niemöller his qualified approval, expressing the opinion that, though the interview contained some dangerously worded passages, it was all to the good that Niemöller had broken away from the conventional formulæ so popular in Western Germany.

From now on, Niemöller's public activities were based more than ever on a principle which he had expressed as follows in his letter to Dr. Heinemann:

> "We and our brethren behind the Iron Curtain belong together and we should not allow any advantages which are offered to us here in the West to induce us to accept the present division of Germany."

For Niemöller this principle was closely connected with the battle for peace. "The Church has the duty to serve in the cause of peace"—that was his conviction and he acted accordingly. Niemöller did not fight in this battle as a dreamer ignorant of the real world but, as another leading German Protestant, Dr. Hans Stempel, the Church President of the Palatinate, once said, he fought "for the very reason that he knew the world". As a Christian he also knew that all Utopian schemes for the improvement of the world were doomed to failure for the reason that human nature cannot be changed for the better. Far from ruling out the attempt, this knowledge made it all the more necessary to try to put Christ's teaching into practice in daily life, particularly that part of it contained in the Sermon on the Mount. "Love your enemies"—had the politicians any right to tear up this fundamental commandment and arbitrarily render it incapable of realization? It was on these lines that Niemöller's attitude to pacifism developed, an attitude that in Germany even in clerical circles frequently provoked smiles of pity or condescension.

When the World Council of Churches gave its official support to "police" action in Korea in 1950, Niemöller signed the declaration in good faith. Some weeks later, when the first reports came through of American planes bombing Korean towns, he regretted having done so. From that moment on, he became a pacifist—not on principle, and not in all situations, but for practical purposes in the present situation. In the course of correspondence with the President of the Pan-European Movement, Graf Coudenhove-Kalergi, in 1956, on the subject of the reunification of Germany, Niemöller called himself a convinced pacifist and anti-militarist. Modern warfare, he wrote, explaining his change from one-time soldier to pacifist, has nothing in common with what was formerly understood by war. War today is a crime. There can be no more just wars. Though pacifism may be a dubious doctrine from the Christian point of view, said Niemöller, he was convinced that, compared with the disaster that the doctrinaire defenders of the principle of waging war might bring about, pacifism was the lesser of two evils. It was a matter of seeing where the greater danger lay—or conversely, which attitude came nearer to the love demanded by Christ. Conversations which Niemöller had during these years with leading German atom physicists, confirmed him in his opinion that war was more than ever before a crime.

Shortly before the World Conference of Churches in Evanston, U.S.A., in the summer of 1954, at which President Eisenhower called on those present to pray for peace, Professor Hahn, the pioneer of German physics, told Niemöller that it remained only to solve certain technical problems and the Earth could be rendered uninhabitable.

Niemöller concluded from this state of affairs that the only way to avoid a third world war was to prevent an armament race between the two main groups of nations. He had never believed there was any truth in the saying, *Si vis pacem, para bellum*—"If you wish for peace, prepare for war"—for history seemed to show that large-scale preparations for war, whatever their intention, invariably led to an explosion. In the present situation it was of paramount importance that Germany be kept out of the competitive rearmament of the Great Powers, and Germany's task consisted in forming a bridge between the two hostile worlds, without identifying itself with the Americans or the Russians, the West or the East. The much talked of crusade for the so-called Christian Occident would, in Niemöller's opinion, be just as much a crime as any other form of war. In any case, what did the term "Christian Occident" mean? Niemöller saw it as a mere weapon of propaganda in the political and ideological conflicts of the time. "In fact we in the Christian Occident are not 'Christian' at all. Our political conceptions are not based on Christ and Christianity, but on Roman imperialism. And what we are witnessing at the moment is an attempt to maintain the hegemony of the White Man by means of force. This attempt will and must fail."

The policy of armed strength Niemöller and his friends opposed with the policy of discussion. Discussion was necessary despite the existence of the Iron Curtain, even though it was a boring and uncomfortable business. Prevailing political opinion, however, favoured the policy of strength, hoping to preserve peace by building up armaments and forcing Russia to her knees. Anyone daring to speak of a neutral Germany in 1950 was branded in the Federal Republic as an idiot or a traitor. Nevertheless Niemöller had the courage to incur that odium, to do what he was convinced every Christian ought to do in the circumstances: he intervened between the contesting parties. When the usual weapon employed against dissidents was brought into action against him, and he was accused of being a fellow-traveller and even a Communist—when he was compared to the Red Dean of Canterbury—Niemöller was not intimidated, but replied: "I am not a Communist and will never become a Communist!" But he added: "We did not capitulate in order to get a third world war!" Then he explained why he had no alternative but to enter the sphere of politics as a layman, a pastor and a complete non-expert: "If I persist in expressing my opinions on political questions, I do so as a Christian who feels compelled, and in duty bound, to do all in his power to avert the unspeakable suffering which threatens the many millions of people in Germany, Europe and the rest of the world. Everything possible must be done, or at least seriously attempted, to prevent a third world war!"

Yet Niemöller knew well that, as a representative of the Church, he was in fact performing "an alien function", as he called it. It was necessary as it had been once before, during the Hitler régime, "for the sake of humanity that otherwise might be in danger of losing the ability to be human". Those people who, in his opinion, were responsible for bringing Germany to the verge of a third world war so soon after the end of the Second were not spared: "It would appear to be difficult to find politicians who pursued a worse policy than those of the years 1945 to 1949. They will not be sacrificing one jot of their dignity, therefore, in accepting the advice of a pastor."

Niemöller looked on the plan to include the German Federal Republic in the western defence organization as a particularly dangerous aspect of this "bad" policy, for it could not fail to provoke a similar move in the east and hence would bring appreciably nearer the prospect of German fighting against German, and Niemöller spoke against it with the same fervour as he had once argued against the creation of "pseudo-States" on either side of the Iron Curtain.

For some years, until the end of 1950, Niemöller's campaign against competitive rearmament enjoyed the approval of the Evangelical Church. The Declaration of Eisenach (July, 1948): "the world needs love, not force", and its completion by the

Bethel Synod (January, 1950) was effectively underlined by the Synod at Berlin-Weissensee in April, 1950. Into the incipient controversy over West German rearmament this Synod, which was held in the Soviet sector of Berlin, had thrown its question: "What can the Church do for peace?" and issued a warning against a continuation of competitive rearmament: "We implore the governments and representatives of our people to allow no power in the world to induce them to accept the illusion that another war could provide the solution to or bring about a change for the better in our distress. . . ."

At the end of August, the Council of the Evangelical Church meeting in Essen had stated with all clarity: "We cannot subscribe to the remilitarization of Germany, either in the West or the East." The Council of Brethren of the Confessing Church had added: "It must remain unthinkable that German should ever shoot at German!" But when the Council of the Evangelical Church met in November, 1950, in the Berlin suburb of Spandau, Niemöller was compelled to realize that the same unanimity no longer prevailed on this vital question. Though the Council stressed in its communiqué that the unity of the Church remained, despite strong tensions, as solid as ever, it went on to say: "The Council realizes that the community of Faith does not include a uniformity of political opinion. The question of whether some form of armament is unavoidable can in Faith receive many different answers." This sentence meant no more, no less—despite its cautious and diplomatic phraseology—than that the position taken up at Essen had now been abandoned. The official Church was handing over the question of remilitarization to the governments concerned. For the first time Niemöller had failed to secure the adoption of his views by the Council, and on a question of decisive importance to him. How had this happened? How was it that some churchmen now rejected views which a few months before they had thought right?

The reasons why the Evangelical Church had at first rejected all suggestion of West German rearmament, then given it qualified approval and finally almost welcomed it, can be understood only in relation to the political situation at that time and to the fateful decisions which were crowded into so comparatively short a period. The events of those few weeks were to influence the future for many years to come, and once again the majority of churchmen were against him when Niemöller expressed the fear that they would lead the German people to disaster. During those autumn days filled with hectic political negotiation and lobbying, the public suddenly awoke to the fact that West Germany was to be re-armed. Though the decision had, no doubt, long since been taken, it came as a complete surprise to the man-in-the-street, as it did to many highly placed individuals in the Bonn Government. When it transpired that the Federal Chancellor, Dr. Adenauer, had suggested West German rearmament to the Americans entirely on his own initiative and without consulting his ministers even, let alone parliament, a heated argument developed, at a cabinet meeting, between him and Dr. Heinemann, the Minister of the Interior, ending with the latter's resignation. Like Niemöller, Heinemann was firmly opposed to German rearmament and his conscience forbade him to remain a member of a government that made decisions on such a vital matter in so high-handed and arbitrary a fashion.

It was at this stage in developments that Niemöller felt it his duty to speak. On 4 October, 1950, he addressed an open letter to Dr. Adenauer accusing him of introducing rearmament without the authorization of parliament, and demanding fresh elections on the grounds that the present Federal Assembly had no mandate from the electorate to vote on that issue. In reply, Dr. Adenauer inquired through his private secretary whether Niemöller had written the letter on his own initiative as a private citizen or in his official capacity, representing a body of opinion within the Evangelical Church. Niemöller's answer—likewise made through his secretary—was that the letter, as clearly indicated by the heading, had been written on his own initiative and in his own name and not on behalf of any third party.

There the matter rested. No detailed reply forthcoming from the Federal Chancellor, Niemöller then addressed a second open letter on the same subject to the American High Commissioner in Germany, Mr. John McCloy. A few days previously, the latter had stated over the radio that the western Allies realized that a German contribution to the defence of Europe would be possible and desirable only if the German people gave it their approval and active support. Niemöller thanked the High Commissioner for this encouraging assurance and asked for further information regarding American intentions. "Many Germans in Western Germany," he wrote, "are increasingly receiving the impression that our people are being misused for purposes against which they believed themselves protected by the Federal Constitution and the Occupation Statute." There was no reply to this letter, either, though the High Commissioner conveyed to Niemöller, privately, his assurance that he had been in earnest when he had said that the German people themselves must decide on the question of rearmament.

Once again Niemöller was in the public eye. Many people were grateful to him for having helped—"in the name of humanity"—to penetrate the veil which the politicians had drawn over their plans for rearmament. Others considered that he had once more shown himself to be the *enfant terrible* of the Church. The Social Democratic Party of Germany, still at that time led by Dr. Adenauer's embittered opponent, Kurt Schumacher, welcomed Niemöller's initiative, though it remains open to question to what extent that party would have agreed with his motives, prompted as they had been by Christian faith rather than political doctrine.* Several meetings took place

---

* How little understanding many groups in this party had for Niemöller, the Christian, is shown, not only by the reaction of local party offices to his declaration regarding de-Nazification, but also by the following, from the S.P.D. newspaper *Neue Vorwärts* dated 25 January, 1952. Strangely enough, the sentiments are very similar to those expressed by Niemöller's opponents in the Christian Democratic Union. "*For ecclesiastical circles to concern themselves with such questions as rearmament is open to objection as unwarrantable interference, while from the religious point of view it savours somewhat of the crank. . . .*"

between Niemöller and the leader of the party, and the Council of Brethren of the Confessing Church held a seven-hour conference with other leading personalities in the S.P.D., reaching the conclusion that only a newly elected Federal Assembly could claim to speak for the people on this question.

It was not surprising, however, that Niemöller should come under severe criticism from those who associated themselves with the official policy of Washington and Bonn, particularly when soon afterwards, before an audience comprising some thousands of Evangelical parishioners, he mentioned the West German Federal Chancellor and Otto Grotewohl, the Prime Minister of the Russian Zone in the same breath. As on many previous occasions, the American-controlled newspaper, *Neue Zeitung*, was the mouthpiece of these critics when it called Niemöller's action a "stab in the back of the Chancellor and the Bonn policy".

It was also to be expected that the general mood of criticism would convey itself to the Church. It found expression at the joint meeting of the Church Conference and the Council of the Evangelical Church on 18 November in Spandau. To use Niemöller's paradoxically military phrase, he withstood a "barrage" for twelve whole hours. There was plenty of plain speaking, but a semblance of unanimity was achieved in a communiqué that attempted to do justice to both sides. In this, the Council declared that it recognized Niemöller's seriousness of purpose in raising the question of rearmament, that it regretted the form his criticisms of the Federal Chancellor had taken and asked all dignitaries of the Church to exercise restraint in their political utterances.

Similar results arose from a meeting of the Hessen-Nassau Synod which took place shortly afterwards in Frankfurt-am-Main. For several days discussion revolved round the question of how far a leading churchman should go in his public utterances. Here, too, Niemöller was subjected to a "barrage" of criticism, which he was not slow to answer. Once again he asserted that an attempt to re-arm Germany would end in cataclysm, "—and to forestall that attempt I am prepared to risk everything". He repeated his opinion that the Church would be neglecting its duty if it did not define its attitude to such vital questions as rearmament. He would, he assured the conference, voice his opinions in the "Fourth Reich" as loudly as he had done in the Third. At one moment, when a speaker held up a certain type as an exemplary "Prince of the Church", Niemöller lost patience, replying: "If you want the sort of man you describe as the Leader of the Church, then that means that you are emulating the Catholic Church. Martin Luther would be ashamed to hear you mention his name. . . ." When another speaker criticized his violence, Niemöller performed a considerable feat of self-criticism in quoting a line from Schiller's drama, *William Tell*: "If I were circumspect, my name would not be Tell!"

This Synod also adopted, by 97 votes to 54, a recommendation urging churchmen to exercise the "greatest possible restraint" in their public statements and to avoid all unnecessary acrimony. More important from Niemöller's point of view, his own Synod affirmed the right of Church officials to express an opinion on political questions. At the same time, the Hessen-Nassau Synod referred back a resolution of the Lutheran Synod of Hanover, which accused Niemöller of having exceeded in his political utterances the bounds of restraint imposed on him by his high ecclesiastical office. In their reference-back, the Synod issued a strongly worded statement which was published in the Press:

> "The Church Synod has taken note of the resolution of the Provincial Synod of the Evangelical Lutheran Provincial Church. The Church Synod rejects the right claimed by the Synod of another Church to express an opinion on the manner in which an official appointed by the Church Synod of Hessen-Nassau performs his duties."

Even for the layman in Church affairs, this duel between the two Synods casts a flood of light on the situation then prevailing among German Protestants. The stage had apparently been reached when they no longer felt any inhibition in passing public censure on one another for wrong and allegedly "right" behaviour! This was the situation against which the American, Ewart E. Turner, an old friend of Niemöller and of the Confessing Church, had warned his German friends before he left their country. "The German Evangelical Church," he said, "ought to take thought lest it disintegrate after the manner of the American Churches in the middle of the nineteenth century. In the South the clergy quoted the Bible to justify the system of slavery, while in the North other passages in the Bible and the spirit of Holy Scripture were being cited in support of its abolition. A somewhat similar situation now prevails among the Christian Churches in the world in regard to war. . . ."

Turner had spoken in 1945, and five years later his words sounded almost prophetic. For now Evangelical Churches in Germany were quoting the Bible, and not only those texts that called on mankind to live together in peace, but also those which seemed to permit a "just" war, crusades of good men against bad and, as a prelude to the fighting—rearmament. The old differences that had arisen during the Hitler régime revived and were argued with high feeling. As previously, controversy centred round the oft quoted passage in St. Paul's letter to the Romans: "Let every soul be subject unto the higher powers. For there is no power but of God: the powers that be are ordained of God," and round the question, "Was a Christian justified at any time in resisting the State?"

Niemöller himself, by temperament and education anything but a revolutionary, had always considered active resistance to the State to be a problematical question. "I myself, for example, would not have taken part as a Christian in the attempt on 20 July on Hitler's life, though I do not wish in any way to detract from the claim of those who did to be considered as valuable and high-minded Christians. My own answer to the question is that I accept the authority of the State as such whatever the circumstances and that I would only refrain from obeying it if it called on me to do something which, according to my lights as a Christian, appeared to me to be contrary to the clearly expressed will of God.

"I know, of course, that the recognition of what *is* God's will is a difficult matter and that this subjective recognition often does not come in a way that enables us to say with a clear conscience and absolute certainty, I *ought not* to do this, or I *ought* to do that."

As in the years following 1933, Niemöller believed that, in the question now at issue, he had this clear conscience and absolute certainty. A speech which he made at the Hamburg Synod in April, 1951, gave some of his audience the impression that the storm that followed his letter to the Federal Chancellor had tired him. But those who spoke of his journey to Canossa rejoiced too soon. Niemöller hastened to assure them that he had in no way made a "vow of political abstinency", but on the contrary would continue to define his attitude to political questions. Meanwhile, it had never been his intention to bring about the fall of the Federal Chancellor.

A correspondence which Niemöller had a few weeks later with the President of the Republic, Dr. Heuss, showed that he was in no mood to retract the statements in his open letters. Once more, the subject under discussion was rearmament. Niemöller begged Heuss, whom he respected as a good Evangelical Christian, "to use his whole influence in the interests of truth and of the German people to ensure that steps were taken to discover the real opinion of the population of Western Germany and that due weight should be given to it in reaching a final decision".

Dr. Heuss replied in a long and factual letter by return of post. He considered Niemöller's arguments in detail, but disagreed that a plebiscite, for example, would be in the interests of internal or external pacification. "Such things are a form of self-deception," he wrote, "based on a false appreciation of the moral and material balance of power at the present time."

Well intentioned and sincere though they were, the political arguments contained in the President's letter could not shake Niemöller's conviction that the policy so stubbornly pursued by the Great Powers and their satellites was dangerously mistaken. Neither could they persuade him to silence the voice of conscience in face of "the moral and material balance of power at the present time." Whenever his duties as Church President and Head of the Church Foreign Department allowed him he therefore continued his campaign for peace. Among the foreign journeys which he undertook in 1951, that to Zagreb deserves particular mention. There he was elected to the committee of a great international peace conference and was the moving spirit behind an appeal addressed to America and the Soviet Union calling on them to take more active steps than hitherto to prevent a third world war. In London also, at a meeting of the Union for Democratic Control, he spoke emphatically against German rearmament. Then came another visit to the United States, to the accompaniment of a grotesque incident planned, probably, by influential political circles as a rejoinder to Niemöller's opposition to the American project of West German rearmament. The immigration authorities refused Frau Niemöller an entry permit on the grounds that, like the majority of Germans, she had been a member of the entirely unpolitical Reich Civil Air Defence Organization. The American Secretary of State, Acheson, evidently disapproved of the action for he intervened personally to secure Frau Niemöller a permit.

It was of great assistance to Niemöller that in this period of his life Karl Barth, the Swiss theologian, invariably sided with him on most questions of the day. When Western Germany entered the European Defence Organization, Professor Barth called the event "the most grievous political error since the 'peace' of Munich," and publicly stressed his "one hundred per cent" agreement with Niemöller and Heinemann. He also frankly declared his attitude in regard to co-operating with the Communists in the cause of peace. "I do not associate myself with the Communist peace-talkers because their opposition to recent developments, though resolute, is not honest. On the other hand, as the house is already on fire, I would rather be seen in the company of the Communists, that is, I would choose to extinguish the fire by any available means rather than fold my hands and reflect how, as a good Christian, one might once again hold this opinion, or that opinion."

At a time when the Communist witch-hunter, Senator McCarthy, was at the height of his power in the United States, such statements as Barth's were bound to arouse violent criticism. But it was as nothing compared with the storm which arose in the last few days of 1951 when the surprise announcement was made that Church President Niemöller, Head of the Foreign Department of the German Evangelical Church and member of the Executive Committee of the World Council of Churches had flown to Moscow at the invitation of the Patriarch to visit the Russian Orthodox Church.*

Niemöller welcomed the invitation for many reasons. A personal visit to the Patriarch Alexius might help to renew the contact between the Russian Church and the other Churches of Christendom that had been broken off since the Amsterdam World Conference of Churches in 1948, and which Niemöller had been trying to renew ever since. At the same time, he hoped to obtain a clearer picture of the Church's position under Soviet Communism and, by no means least, he intended to do his utmost while in Moscow to secure the release and repatriation

---

* The attempts to depict Niemöller and his friends as Communists reached a climax in June, 1950, after Niemöller had declared on a number of occasions that "it is an infamous distortion of the truth to tell us that the Church would be destroyed if the Communists came." He promised to pay a million marks to anyone who could prove to him that armed resistance to Communism was justified by Holy Scripture. "The Communists are human beings like the rest of us to whom we must preach the glad Tidings. Perhaps Christ would say today, 'It is easier for the Communists and the whores to enter the Kingdom of Heaven than for you.'"

of those thousands of German prisoners-of-war still in Russia.

It might have been expected that this first visit of a prominent non-Communist individual from Western Germany to the Soviet Union to take place since the end of the Second World War would be followed by politicians with interest and attention, though naturally with reserve, for in the last resort the maintenance of world peace depended on the restoration to normality of the disturbed relations between East and West. The first reaction to the news of Niemöller's visit was, however, very different. Once again, as so often before, he had to submit to being called a heretic, a traitor or simply a fool by a large section of what was called "public opinion", for the sole reason that he had dared to swim against the current of accepted prejudice.

The first to express his disapproval was the Federal Chancellor, Dr. Adenauer. "I find it most regrettable," he said, "that a German in the position of Church President Martin Niemöller should choose to stab his own government in the back in this fashion and at this time." Niemöller's reply to this attack, which Dr. Adenauer's former Minister of the Interior, Dr. Heinemann, called a "defamation in typical Fascist style", left nothing to be desired as regards clarity. "The Evangelical Church does not allow any worldly authority to prescribe what it should do or not do."

A telegram from the Federal Committee of the Young German Democrats was rich in the jargon of the political arena: "Serve peace and stay in Moscow. Your return is not desired before the last prisoner-of-war has been repatriated." The telegram was on about the same level as the placard which Niemöller found affixed to his house on his return: "Back to Moscow, Tovarich Niemöller!" Most newspapers commented in similar style. "Ambassador without a Mission"—"Moscow's Stooge"—"Stalin's Trojan Horse"—"Pastor or Politician?" Those are only a selection of the headlines offered to readers. Many Social Democrats even, who apparently were beginning

Hertha Niemöller

to fear competition from Niemöller's like-minded friend, Dr. Heinemann, suddenly cooled in their affections and spoke of Niemöller's "self-appointed journeys in search of the limelight" and the "extraordinary harm" which they caused.

The Chairman of the Council of the Evangelical Church, Bishop Dibelius, came to Niemöller's defence in the midst of this welter of calumny and misunderstanding, strongly condemning the "senseless rumours" and "gross inaccuracies" with which the Western Press speeded the parting traveller. "His journey has nothing whatever to do with politics; it is his opponents who have made it political. Was that necessary? One ought really to have greater respect for his high purpose."

The ten days which Niemöller spent in Moscow accompanied by his daughter, Hertha, as interpreter, supplied a wealth of impressions and brought him some considerable success. In the course of lengthy discussion, he was able to induce the Patriarch Alexius and the Metropolitan Nikoley to agree to take part in the world ecclesiastical talks and also to take up closer relations with the Evangelical Church in Germany. He preached a sermon to a congregation of two thousand Baptists who waved their handkerchiefs in farewell when he left, and at a midnight service in Moscow Cathedral the Patriarch led his German guest—a great honour!—behind the iconostasis and allowed him to share in the liturgically most impressive service from there. More important than all this: Niemöller gained the realization that a strong and vital religious life prevailed in the Soviet Union. "The Russian Orthodox Church is very much alive and anything but moribund. I could only wish that churches in Germany were as full." Niemöller was allowed also to visit German working families. He had a long conversation with the Deputy Foreign Minister, Sorin, on the subject of prisoners-of-war, and found the Russian a sympathetic listener. A lively discussion took place with the All-Russia Peace Committee. During its course one of the members called out angrily to Niemöller: "The Germans killed twelve million people here in

Russia, and now you start haggling over the 13,000 prisoners-of-war we are keeping as war criminals!"

"At that moment I was once again a whipped dog for my beloved German people," said Niemöller in the lectures he gave on his Russian visit, in different parts of the world during the first six months of 1952. These included his fifth lecture-tour of the United States. The haggling was not entirely unsuccessful and some months after Niemöller's visit the Russians did in fact repatriate 800 German prisoners-of-war and internees.

"Leave me in peace!" said Niemöller on his return from Moscow to the pressmen at the Berlin airport. He was wearing a tall fur cap which he had bought in Moscow and which he changed for an ordinary hat when the plane took off again for Frankfurt. In honour of his Moscow host, he was also wearing the golden cross and chain which the Patriarch Alexius had given him as a parting gift.

The attacks made on him in the Press and elsewhere after his return were, according to Niemöller, so childish that he prefers to pass them over in silence. The Russian officials who welcomed him in Moscow, he says, had apparently understood better than those in Germany that his visit was purely concerned with Church affairs. When some members of the Hessen-Nassau Synod attempted to revive the political reproach, Niemöller replied in words which clearly reflected his bitterness of feeling: "If I am not to be allowed to speak and act in my office as I must speak and act as a Christian, then take my office, dear friends, and I wish you joy of it. But see you don't fail in it. I have no wish to fail in my ecclesiastical office, but wish to be allowed to act as a Christian!"

The public in their incomprehension left Niemöller no peace. Repeatedly during the following months he felt obliged to raise the question: "Are we still capable of thinking without prejudice? It looks as though there were a secret conspiracy afoot whereby only such news was allowed to reach the world from behind the Iron Curtain as made all attempt at a *rapproche-*

ment seem a foolish dream, even a crime against humanity. Yet we know that a war with the eastern world would mean the certain and complete destruction of the German people and probably of all European peoples. . . . I have held it to be my *duty as a Christian* to tell the people in Moscow that, in my opinion, not only do the peoples of Western Europe not want another war, but there is not one millionaire in the whole of America who would not gladly sacrifice his entire wealth if by so doing he could avert the catastrophe. I shall also not conceal the fact, when I visit America, that the impression I gained during my stay in Moscow was that no one there, either, desires a third world war. People may smile and shrug their shoulders at this, but as a Christian and as a human being I am determined to leave nothing that lies within my power undone in order to inspire the rulers of the world with the courage to go on trying to reach an understanding. The lives of millions of human beings are at stake and no Christian can afford to say: 'What have they to do with me?' "

There is a danger that in attempting to trace the course of Niemöller's life since his liberation from the concentration camp, the biographer may concentrate on the most outstanding events and thereby overlook the amount of steady routine work which Niemöller performed as President of the Hessen-Nassau Church, and as head of the Foreign Affairs Department of the Evangelical Church. This would be unjust, for even during the times of violent controversy Niemöller took scrupulous care not to neglect the day-to-day duties of office, for the performance of which his foreign travels provided a constant stimulus. That was particularly the case with his six-week stay in India in the winter of 1952/3. The purpose of the visit was to attend the World Conference of Christian Youth in Travancore and also two sessions of the World Council of Churches. Once again, Niemöller was accompanied by his wife. The most important result of this, his first visit to India, was the realization that a genuine comparison was possible between Gandhi-ism and Christianity.

"Who actually lives the teaching of Jesus better, the so-called Christian who seeks a thousand excuses to dodge the commandments of Jesus, or the Hindu, the 'heathen', who does not recognize Jesus as the Son of God, but nevertheless makes every effort to live according to his precepts?... Can there be Christianity without Christ? Then Gandhi-ism is that Christianity." In the summer of 1953 at the Assembly of the German Evangelical Church, Niemöller once more took up this theme and applied it to present-day Germany. "Gandhi was quite simply right when he insisted that in no case and in no circumstances should his people resort to force if they were to fulfil their task as a people among peoples. Should we not listen to this warning and take it to heart before murder and fratricide starts once again?"

In India Niemöller also began to appreciate the significance of the racial problem. After his visit he was to place it side by side with East-West relationships in the forefront of many of his speeches and articles. He became convinced that world leadership was in process of passing from the white races to the coloured, and he urged that no effort should be spared to ensure that the coloured peoples did not use it for purposes of revenge. To come to terms with the coloured peoples, he said, was not only in accordance with Christian duty, but with the dictates of good sense. True to these views Niemöller signed an appeal while he was in India, addressed to the United Nations by the World Council of Churches at its meeting in the North Indian town of Lucknow, in which it called for an improvement of social conditions in Asia before they led to strife.

On 6 September, 1953, the population of Western Germany re-elected Dr. Adenauer's government by a large majority, thus expressing approval of his policy of "strength". Niemöller interpreted the results of the elections in the following words: "By voting in this way the electorate has abandoned its power to assist in the peaceful re-unification of our Fatherland." Some few weeks previously, while Niemöller had been on holiday in

During his visit to India in the summer of 1953 this photograph was taken when Niemöller and Dr. Visser 't Hooft, Secretary-General of the Council of Churches, were in conversation with Mr. Jawaharlal Nehru, Prime Minister of India the Black Forest, the newspapers had published an election appeal in which he accused the Federal Government of having acted in disregard of popular opinion. He had also—much to the annoyance of Evangelical politicians of the Christian Democratic Union, among them, Dr. Ehlers, the President of the Bundestag, who accused him of breaking the neutrality of the Church—called on all those political groups to unite who "favour a complete re-orientation of German foreign policy without one-sided economic or military commitments to West or East, and who are determined to pursue a German policy of re-unification and peace".

Like that of his friend Dr. Heinemann's "United German People's Party" founded in the previous year, Niemöller's election appeal failed to gain supporters. To the Hessen-Nassau Synod Niemöller again became a "case". A motion of censure put before the Synod in reference to the election appeal was defeated by 74 votes to 50, but the Synod took note that Niemöller had disregarded a resolution passed on 29 November, 1950, in which it had called on the clergy to exercise the greatest possible restraint in political utterances. Niemöller himself did not attend the meeting of the Synod.

Meanwhile, in the autumn of 1953, Niemöller continued his work, unconcerned whether his actions were approved or not. Further travels abroad took him to Budapest, Prague and Evanston, Illinois. There was no lack of urgent business to attend to, though the internal situation in the Church often made work unnecessarily difficult. Since the differences of opinion revealed in Spandau in November, 1950, on the question of rearmament had re-opened the old rifts within the Church, the latter had continued to widen until now the German Evangelical Church threatened to split into two opposing factions. Ten leaders of the Church, most of them members of the Confessing Church, the Lutheran Bishops Lilje (Hanover), Meiser (Bavaria), Wurm (Württemberg) and Stählin (Oldenburg) being among their number, had published in March, 1952, a document setting forth their attitude to the question: "Military Service and the Christian Conscience." In direct contrast to Niemöller they stressed that it was the duty of a Christian to defend, if necessary with his life, the "values" of western civilization. The Press was already beginning to speak of the "isolation" of Niemöller and his friends when Bishop Meiser, at that time senior Lutheran Bishop in Germany, issued a further statement to the effect that the Church which he represented would have complete sympathy with the motives of those citizens who resolved to contribute to military preparedness for patriotic reasons. The question, he said, of rearmament or no rearmament was a matter of personal opinion and, therefore, not one which concerned the Christian conscience.

Concurrently with these statements, steps were being undertaken to remove Niemöller from his appointment as Head of the Church's Foreign Affairs Department. The methods employed were, from the start, under no less criticism in ecclesiastical circles than those used at the Synod of Espelkamp in the spring of 1955 to unseat the President of the Synod, Dr. Heinemann. In both cases the campaign was started by the same man, Bishop Herntrich (who died in September, 1958), who was then a member of the Hamburg High Consistory, in Niemöller's case at the Lutheran General Synod in Weimar, where Herntrich declared that, as run by Niemöller, the Foreign Department was not fulfilling its functions adequately. At the same time the Synod called for the "radical reorganization" of the Department. In protest against this defamation Niemöller then resigned his appointments on the Council of the Evangelical Church. Though upon investigation the charges levelled against him proved to be without foundation, intrigues continued until, in June, 1956, the Council dismissed him from office "in absentia". No reason was given and the Council acted against the protests of 240 theologians who, a few weeks previously, had called on the Evangelical Church not to send a man into the wilderness whose reputation throughout Christendom was so incomparably great. Amongst these theologians were men from Holland, France, Belgium, Denmark, South Africa and Switzerland.

Niemöller himself reacted to the behaviour of his brothers and colleagues in Christ with surprising calm, at the same time publicly affirming that he had been the victim of a "militant Confessionalism". In a letter to one of the big German newspapers he stated that a matter of Church politics had been involved in his dismissal. He had been baptized in the Lutheran Church, confirmed a Lutheran and ordained a Lutheran. What distinguished him from his successor was the fact that he was not a member of the United Evangelical-Lutheran Church of Germany, but that as a Lutheran theologian he was President of a united Church. He had, as he said, the wrong ecclesiastical "Party Book". He regretted that attempts were being made to conceal this, the real reason for his dismissal, for "when differences arise we ought to fight them out openly and honestly". He therefore indignantly rejected the "warm thanks" for his services which were conveyed to him on behalf of the official Church. What sort of "thanks" could be reconciled with the kind of treatment he had received . . . ?

The United Evangelical-Lutheran Church of Germany contested on a number of occasions Niemöller's assertion that he had been a victim of their militant Confessionalism and their political tendencies and they denied having raised any demands that the conduct of the Foreign Affairs Department should be in the hands of one of their members. "The United Evangelical-Lutherans do not play at power politics," they said in a letter published by the Frankfurter *Allgemeine Zeitung* on 12 July, 1956, "and it is desirable that this error should not be perpetuated." On the other hand, the Munich paper, *Süddeutsche Zeitung* had published four months previously, in March of that year, a report from Hanover, one of the strongholds of Lutheranism, to the effect that, for two years past, the Lutherans had been trying to fill the office of Head of the Foreign Affairs Department with one of their members, for the reason that the

German communities abroad which were administered by that Department in the sphere of Church affairs were 80 per cent Lutheran.

Niemöller's composure over the whole affair lacked any trace of bitterness. Objectively as a doctor assessing a clinical report he wrote a memorandum carefully analysing every detail in the "case" which his opponents had brought against him. In conversation with him it was almost possible to detect a certain relief that he was now free to devote himself to other tasks which called for no regard to factional feeling or Church politics. Moreover, in or out of office, he had lost none of his friends abroad, as the spate of invitations to visit various countries showed, invitations which he gladly accepted whenever his duties as President of the Hessen-Nassau Church allowed. Nothing, at any rate, in his work or manner of life suggested that he was going to allow himself to be shunted into a siding. On the contrary, particularly in the recent past, he has repeatedly singled out the weak spots in official Church policy with astonishing accuracy, and to many observers the justification of his criticisms has been supplied by the degree of anger which they have provoked. When, for example, in his New Year sermon on 1 January, 1957, Niemöller made some perfectly serious comments on the Pope's Christmas Message, the reaction on the part of Roman Catholics surprised even him in the intensity of its abuse.

Niemöller had said: "a man claiming to speak as Christ's Deputy on Earth" had conceded to the United Nations the right to anticipate any attack impending by one state upon another, in other words, had conceded the right to conduct a preventive war. At the same time he had declared that a Christian could not refuse to perform military service on grounds of conscience. "Here," said Niemöller, "the authority of Christ is invoked against the interests of truth, here Christ's name has been misused. Christ," he went on, "had said—and all Christians should know it—'Blessed are the meek, for they shall inherit

190

the earth! Blessed are the peace-makers for they shall be called the sons of God!' "

The Catholic News Agency described these remarks as a "monstrous insult to Pope Pius XII". A Würzburg newspaper spoke of "diabolical conceit" which in the last resort was a matter for psychologists, "but in Niemöller's case psychologists have long since given him up, declaring him to be incurable". Finally, the Catholic newspaper, *Echo der Zeit*, wrote: "If Niemöller imagines he can revive the low-level polemics of the Reformation, he is deceived. We no longer live in an age of scurrilous pamphleteers."

None of these shrill protests could detract from the weight of Niemöller's arguments, however, for none of them attempted to argue in return. The same applied in the spring of 1957 when he warned the Synod of the German Evangelical Church, with all the forcefulness at his command, not to start a ministry among the armed forces, for any such organization would be largely dependent on the State and provide the basis for the creation of a military Church. Niemöller issued his warning in Spandau, which had once been the scene of a radical change in official Church policy, but this time no change took place. The majority of churchmen paid no attention to his warning, though many of those who heard him speak will long remember the question he asked: "What do you intend to preach to the soldiers who are to fire atomic weapons?"

Niemöller spoke then with the voice of an inexorable and incorruptible guardian of the public conscience. The question he then asked shows what the public has to expect from this man who, for as long as he is spared to Christendom and to the German people, will remain a great force in the background, alike honoured and feared. That he arouses fear was shown by a question asked in a national newspaper: "Who runs West German foreign policy, the Foreign Minister, or Niemöller?" That he is also respected was demonstrated by a speech given in the Bonn Assembly, by a deputy of the highest reputation, during a debate on reactionary tendencies in the new West German Navy. Professor Carlo Schmid (Social Democrat) declared in the debate on 18 April, 1956:

"If we are going to mention names, would not Admiral Graf Spee be a more worthy model for the German Navy (applause from the whole House) and—you can say what you like—a man like Niemöller, who has been a courageous naval officer and later fought with no less courage against inhumanity? (Applause from the Social Democrats.) He, too, seems to me a better model than Dönitz. Now I am not talking about the political opinions of Herr Niemöller—that is quite another matter, though there and elsewhere he has proved himself a man. (Renewed applause from the Social Democrats.) As long as officers believe they might have to answer to Dönitz for entering the service of the Federal Republic, they are not living in the spirit which must animate our Federal Forces if they are to lead an honourable existence. And they will only do that if the spirit of humanity, of human decency and human rights, is not merely mentioned in service regulations, but practised actively, day-in, day-out (Applause), for without that spirit the bravest of bravery is no virtue, not even a military virtue."

Admittedly it will not be easy to blaze a trail through the jungle in which the German Evangelical Church finds itself at the present time. Whatever men may be found to help it to do so, it is to be hoped that Niemöller will be among the first. For —despite all his faults, which he has like any other man—he understands many things which many so-called churchmen and pious Christians have either never understood or long since forgotten. Above all, Niemöller knows that the Church exists for *all* men, for the oppressed and those deprived of their rights, and also for the evildoers, and that its chief concern should be, not to defend the existing order or strive to achieve a new one, but to keep on reminding an all too confident humanity of the doubtfulness and transitoriness of all "solutions" to our problems. Finally, the Church should remember that whenever it becomes too concerned for its own existence, its reputation, its power and its good relations with the rulers of the State, at that moment it is in the greatest danger of failing in its task. Because he sees and understands this, Niemöller may well remain a member of that select band who are called to be pastors— pastors, and not princes of the Church.

Chapter Nine

PERSONAL PORTRAIT

SOME readers may consider that a serious and objective bio-graphy would have done better to avoid colouring the story with the anecdotal and purely personal touch. In any attempt to trace the life of a contemporary against the background of con-temporary events, the introduction of too much incidental detail must, surely, blur and confuse the main outline of the story, be-sides introducing a suggestion of hero worship—or its opposite —and thus sail perilously near the reef on which so many well meant biographies have foundered.

It would be foolish to deny that this danger exists, but would not something be lacking in the portrayal of the character of the man, Niemöller, complex and elusive as it is, if all minor in-cidents of his private and domestic life were omitted?

Anyone glancing at Martin Niemöller's diary of appoint-ments during the last ten years could not fail to be overcome with a mixture of awe and admiration, and indeed, the amount of work which this man manages to get through per hour and per day would seem almost uncanny if one did not know the rapidity and precision with which he is accustomed to think and make decisions, and, in particular, if the mainspring of his almost inhuman passion for work were not apparent. Though he himself perhaps is not aware of the fact except at odd mo-ments, those eight years which he lost in the concentration camp must undoubtedly exert their effect in an unconscious urge to make up for their comparative inactivity by living at twice the speed of ordinary men. This motive helps to explain his im-patience which many critics have alleged is unworthy of a leader

Pastor and Mrs. Niemöller photographed in Honolulu
in August 1949 while en route to Australia

of the Church, and which always shows itself, for example, when the business at some conference or other does not seem to him to be progressing fast enough, or when some matter which in Niemöller's opinion calls for a simple and rapid decision is thrashed out in long-winded speeches. At such moments Niemöller can become harsh and ill-tempered, even intolerant, and there is no doubt that remarks passed in such moods have made him many enemies.

Naturally, it would be an exaggeration to ascribe Niemöller's inability to contain himself in patience, and his abrupt actions, entirely to those lost eight years—and incidentally, Niemöller himself knows well enough that they were not "lost", but on the contrary were a very salutary period of meditation and gathering of strength. They help to explain the accentuation of certain of his characteristics, which are the very opposite of those associated with "caution", "circumspection", or "tactics". If it were not otiose and lacking in good taste to interpret the life of a churchman by the yardstick of an astrologer, one might almost say that "it was written in the stars" that he should become such a man and that his life should take such a course. An article in a South German newspaper dealing with his horoscope, recognized Niemöller as "a notable moral force in the contemporary world", but it also mentioned his frank and forthright utterances, so often characterized as ruthless and dangerous, as qualities typical of one born under the prevailing influences of Uranus and Mars. Incidentally, Niemöller shares at least one thing with the man he opposes, Konrad Adenauer, namely the sign of the Zodiac, Aries the Ram, as he does with Marcus Porcius Cato (*Ceterum censeo, Carthaginem esse delendam*), the Maid of Orleans, Georgi Malenkov, and P. Mendès-France. "As a prophet of woe," wrote the astrologer, "he sometimes gets on our nerves; but, unfortunately, he is often proved right. . . ."

"He came like a whirlwind," wrote a South-west German newspaper of Niemöller's first post-war visit to his old parish of

Dahlem, "stimulating, refreshing, but also alarming." The qualities which such formulæ imply Niemöller cannot lay aside by merely taking thought, for they are an essential part of himself and often give his words their characteristic flavour—unpalatable though it may sometimes seem.

These qualities have often landed him in trouble, as, for example, after the interview with Hitler, on 25 January, 1934, when the leaders of the Church accused him of having brought about the final rupture with the *Führer* through his lack of forethought. No doubt it was the memory of that time that underlay Dr. Wurm's statement, in 1951, that Niemöller's destructive power was often greater than his constructive abilities. This from an Evangelical bishop about an Evangelical Church President! A similar note was sounded when Dr. Hermann Ehlers, at that time President of the West German Federal Assembly and a former colleague of Niemöller's during the Battle of the Churches, could not refrain from concluding a flattering newspaper article, on the occasion of Niemöller's sixtieth birthday, by mentioning "a sharpness of tone which even his friends find distressing and a highly dangerous lack of foresight and tactics". One could make a long list of similar strongly worded criticisms. "Free-booter of God", "a disruptive and disturbing element", "a man with all the characteristics of hysteria"—right up to the recent past, plenty of effort and imagination has been employed in trying to make this dangerous, disturbing and misunderstood man fit neatly into some pigeon-hole.

Beside unfriendly criticism, however, there has been no lack of sincere efforts to understand Niemöller. A particularly fair assessment is contained in the book of portraits, *It happened in Germany*, by the former Reich Finance Minister, Graf Schwerin von Krosigk: "Niemöller is the movement in the watch of the Evangelical Church. The movement does not show the time, but without it, the watch cannot work." The writer added: "The Evangelical Church must be strong and open hearted enough to allow scope to this man, though he may often be a source of embarrassment . . . for he also brings about the clarification of issues without which it could not exist."

A letter which Niemöller received in 1955 from his former master at Elberfeld Grammar School, Dr. Ernst Brake, then aged over eighty, shows that this "restlessness", which many of those who have to deal with him find so disturbing, was part of his make-up even as a boy: "Even as a boy, dear Martin, you looked to the restlessness of the sea as the scene of your actions. The stormy waves have carried you up and down until now you are on the high seas. May a good star be your guide!"

Niemöller's efforts to leave no minute unfilled, hardly ever to decline an invitation or a challenge to speak, debate or write have caused even some of his more benevolent critics to suggest that he occasionally neglects the "human" side of his work. He ought, such persons say, to give more time to the small things of life, ought to discuss their personal problems more with the pastors of his Church and their wives—and without allowing his glance to stray to his appointments' diary. Underlying feelings of this kind may be the "Pastor's Prayer" that originated and quickly became known in the area administered by the Hessen-Nassau Church. "Lord, protect our Church President! Thou alone knowest where he is . . ."—a reference to Niemöller's frequent journeys abroad, which a just observer would agree often brought incidental benefit to the Hessen-Nassau Church, and to its reputation.

It is certainly no chance that Niemöller has none of those hobbies which occupy the spare time of many other busy men. Niemöller seldom gives himself an evening off, much as he deserves one, and in the words of his chauffeur, his only hobby is work.

His chauffeur ought to know, for he accompanies Niemöller on his frequent and lengthy journeys by car in Germany and sees more of him than does possibly any one other person.

To this hobby called work Niemöller, then, gives first place in his life, though it would be only just to concede that for him it is not, as for so many other men, work for work's sake, but for the sake of preaching the Word of God. Anyone acquainted with Niemöller would think it absurd to try to imagine him taking a leisurely afternoon stroll, or sitting down to elaborate meals at set times, reading the newspaper in a café or sitting over a glass of beer in the evenings with some like-minded cronies, discussing the day's events. For these or similar activities there is no place in his schedule. Each morning he sets out at eight o'clock from Wiesbaden where he lives with his family, to cover the eighteen miles to his office in Darmstadt. With him in the car is usually one of his staff to discuss and receive instructions for the day's work, or sometimes a journalist is invited to share the journey to work out one of those newspaper interviews with Niemöller that strike the public with such explosive effect.

At midday, the members of the Consistory and other employees have a break for lunch in a nearby restaurant, but their chief, as they call him, remains behind in his bare office with his files, his only refreshment some soup which his secretary has prepared for him on a portable electric cooker. When he returns home to Wiesbaden in the evening, he will as like as not find the visitors to whom he has given late appointments already waiting for him. When they have all gone, he will often stay up talking until the early hours with a guest over a bottle of good "church wine"—the Hessen-Nassau Church owns a number of excellent vineyards. At six o'clock next morning, the guest will probably be wakened by the sound of Niemöller's voice monotonously intoning in the adjoining room. That will mean that the pastor, a notorious early riser, is making use of the quiet hours before breakfast to deal with the previous day's correspondence by dictaphone.

Niemöller's daily correspondence is usually bulky and contains letters from abroad as well as from home, mostly on church, religious or political matters. He deals with it all most scrupulously. His secretaries have instructions to show him every letter and never to hold anything back, whatever its contents. Niemöller demands to see everything himself, and at once, and he gets very angry with his staff if he discovers later that some letter has not been shown to him, perhaps because it is offensively critical. Niemöller takes every correspondent seriously, and no letter therefore remains unanswered. In his replies he always tries to give his correspondent the concrete advice he has asked for and not to fob him off with some well meaning but non-committal words. This is not always easy for the subjects on which people seek Niemöller's advice are often very personal ones. For example, a Berlin mother, alarmed by reports of impending West German rearmament, asked him what women could do to prevent another war. Niemöller's detailed reply ended with the statement that if it came to rearmament, his own three sons would refuse to perform military service and accept whatever consequences ensued. "I can only recommend your son to do the same, though I cannot make the decision for him."

Niemöller has to thank the stamina and robust physical health he has inherited from his Westphalian forefathers for the fact that he has been able to continue this life of perpetual strain and restlessness well into his seventh decade without falling prey, like many other men of his generation, to the familiar "managerial disease". Throughout his life he has been spared serious illness, and even the log he kept as a naval cadet reveals a strong constitution. Apart from occasional headaches or muscular strain, an operation for adenoids and an infected wound on his left hand which prevented him going ashore in Barcelona, he remained fit and, what was more, able to go about his duty when most of the others were seasick. Later in life he has suffered now and then from the complaints common to all mortals—coughs, colds, fevers and other minor indispositions. Whenever possible on these occasions, he transfers his office to his sickroom, receives his visitors in bed and tries generally to ensure there is no interruption in the steady flow of work—and the flow continues, incidentally, during the holidays which he manages to combine with preaching or lecture tours or visits to colleagues. Sometimes, admittedly, as he grows older, his heart begins to revolt after a particularly tiring day fortified with too much strong coffee—a stimulus he finds it hard to forgo—or else raised blood-pressure causes him discomfort. In such cases Niemöller prescribes himself his own, well-proven medicine, despite the advice of the family doctor who would, no doubt, prefer to see him take a long rest in bed or go for a walk in the well-tended avenues of the spa town, Wiesbaden. Before joining the family for the evening meal, Niemöller takes the big bottle of Steinhäger, the famous Westphalian gin, from the larder behind the kitchen. It can easily be imagined that a man who resorts to such drastic remedies and survives sometimes takes the illnesses of other people somewhat lightly.

It would be completely wrong to imagine, however, that because he has a passion for work, Niemöller must necessarily be a stern and inhuman robot. He has every appreciation for the pleasures of life, both large and small. That applies as much to "the small boy who ate so much cake", as his wife describes her first impression of him at her parents' house, as it does to the man who knows how to appreciate a good meal, a fine wine and a good quality cigar—though he devotes no more time to these things than absolutely necessary.

It assorts well with these characteristics that in contrast to many dignitaries of the Church, Niemöller sets no store by maintaining an attitude of dignified superiority and a discreet distance between himself and lesser mortals, but enjoys a good laugh and in fact possesses a robust sailor's humour, as his autobiography, *From U-boat to Pulpit*, amply shows.

After he had long since become one of the best-known churchmen in the world, Niemöller was one day being shown the sights of Sydney by an Australian Baptist clergyman. "And this, Brother Niemöller," said the latter, pointing to a hideous, red-brick building, "is the chief blot on our city."

"A blot? How so?" asked Niemöller, imagining the man was referring to the building's appearance.

"It's a brewery!" replied the parson.

"Oh . . . yes . . . I see . . . of course . . . ," said Niemöller, somewhat taken aback by this display of fanatical temperance. Then in a serious voice he added: "You're quite right. Beer really isn't much of a drink. Give me a good whisky any day!"

Fortunately, the Baptist had a sense of humour and took Niemöller's rejoinder in good part, but it requires little imagination to see that such jokes would not be to the taste of many of the clergy. In truth, many of those worthy gentlemen who wear the tightly-buttoned Lutheran cassock and the gold cross on their breasts are not a little shocked by this man. Is it, they ask, seemly for a prince of the Church to say such things, or, dressed only in shorts and shirt, argue with Communists in southern India, when Communists are avoided like the plague by all his more orthodox colleagues? Should he be seen shaking hands with a fellow Christian from the Eastern Zone of Germany when this man is known to disagree with and oppose the official policy of the West? Is it wise to criticize the Pope's Christmas Message as a justification of preventive war and an attempt to interfere with German politics when the "prevailing" opinion favours solidarity between the two big denominations at any price? Should he go to Moscow at a time when public opinion will interpret the trip as virtual treason?

By what he says and does Niemöller makes it abundantly clear that he has no intention of accepting any of the contemporary political, social, economic, cultural or even religious taboos at their face value. He is too much a Protestant in the original sense of the word to conform in these matters for the sake of respectability, convention or even the Church's reputation. This of course makes him unpopular with the orthodox, but his patent sincerity and disinterest, which even his opponents do not challenge, ensure that people listen to him whenever he has something to say. None of the many denigration campaigns, none of the boycotts which have been imposed on him during the course of the years by newspapers of all shades of opinion, have been able to alter this fact. Even when his views seem at first sight far-fetched, Niemöller is listened to. For so often during the last ten years those same views have been proved to be right; in expressing them when he did Niemöller had been ahead of his time. Men who possess that quality of foresight have always been laughed at or feared, and because they disturb their contemporaries the latter invariably attempt to dismiss them by stamping them as "poor fools" or "dangerous dreamers", even while secretly agreeing with them. Niemöller is one of those who has had to get used to this treatment.

It would be wrong to assume, however, that he is indifferent to criticism. The verse stuck on the door of his office in Wiesbaden suggests his vulnerability:

> "*I wish I were an elephant,*
> *Then my luck would be in;*
> *It's not his tusks I envy*
> *But the thickness of his skin.*"

The caricatures which appear in the Press, however malicious, do not worry Niemöller, he has too strong a sense of humour for that. Nor do the numerous jokes about him which go the rounds in Germany.* Downright calumny and abuse he finds harder to take calmly, and this applies above all to attacks by former friends.

During the Battle of the Churches he discovered that friends can become opponents, and after the Second World War the experience became more frequent. It has always caused him considerable distress, for Niemöller himself is accused by his critics of over-simplifying his relationships by applying the labels "friend" or "enemy" to everyone. It gives him all the more

---

* One of the best known is: What is the difference between a missionary and Niemöller? Answer: A missionary makes savages pious, Niemöller makes the pious savage.

pleasure when former opponents become friends. A typical example was the literary editor of a big South-west German newspaper. In 1947 this man was speaking of the "publicity conscious" Niemöller who "is in no way entitled to come forward as the mouthpiece of the new German democracy". Three years later the same man was paying tribute to "Niemöller's iron resolve to hold fast to the spirit of the Christian teaching" and to "his truly great qualities as a fighter". "Is it a crime," continued the writer, "for a theologian to declare spiritual war on an opponent and at the same time reject a preventive war against Russia as un-Christian? . . . It is time that louder voices were raised against this crusade-psychosis which has nothing to do with Christianity."

Here a Saul has become a Paul under the impact of Niemöller's vigorous campaign against rearmament and war. After long hesitation, a man has realized that this controversial pastor is fighting for neither of the great forces opposing one another in the world, but against the abuse and distortion of the Bible.

Niemöller has often been accused of negligence in the choice of his friends and collaborators—for choosing, in short, "false friends". This argument is a favourite one with western politicians who say that in his passionate campaign for peace Niemöller has in effect been doing valuable propaganda for Russia. To Niemöller the problem is non-existent, for he is quite serious in his repeated assertions: "I am not a politician," and he cannot therefore judge his friends by political standards. When he was accused, for example, of supporting Mrs. Roosevelt's and Mr. Morgenthau's thesis of Germany's collective guilt by issuing the Stuttgart Declaration of Guilt in 1945, he could truthfully say that the Declaration had nothing to do with politics, but was a purely Christian matter, as was his more recent visit to Moscow. On the question of "false friends", moreover, his attitude is clear. "Personally I find it preferable to associate with questionable people for a good cause than with the best friends in the world for an unworthy one."

"To associate with questionable people for a good cause"—
this is the kind of provocative and ambiguous statement which
has brought Niemöller much censure, for he says what he thinks
and he means what he says. As a Swiss newspaper has written:
"This quality has cost him dear, but it has also provided him
with an invisible armour which so far has protected him against
snipers from all quarters." There has been no lack of such
snipers during the twenty-five years that Niemöller has been in
the limelight and he might perhaps have averted many of their
attacks if he had shown more caution and tactical sense. But
those are not qualities which he possesses in any marked degree
or which he values. This applies not least to his relations with
the Press. "All I get from the German Press is stabs," he once
said in a moment of bitterness, and no doubt he was thinking
of tendentious news reporting, biased reports of his lectures and
spiteful comments on his foreign travels and activities within the
Church. But to be fair he should have added that, from the
start of his public career, he has had and still has many supporters among journalists, and particularly during his campaign
against rearmament, though he has lost some as a result of his
sometimes unjust strictures on the Press. It is curious that he
should seem unaware of this, for Niemöller's publicity sense is
well above that of most contemporary leaders of the Church,
and he might well have considered a career in journalism at that
time after the First World War when he had not yet chosen the
Church. One could well imagine him using to good effect the
platform offered by a newspaper editorship or a senior post in
broadcasting.

Niemöller had become accustomed to broadcasting early on,
in his Münster years. He quickly lost all nervousness before the
microphone and realized that it would be a mistake to employ
the technique of the pulpit in the more intimate atmosphere of
the studio. When television made its appearance, he was one of
the first churchmen to realize the opportunities which it offered
to the Church. He had his first experience of being televised

when he was in the United States, and he helped to popularize this new medium in the German Church by volunteering to preach the sermon at some of the first attempts made in Germany to televise a church service—and the complicated apparatus used in those days imposed a considerable physical strain on all concerned.

Niemöller also welcomes the film as an adjunct to radio and television in reaching ever wider audiences. It was on his advice that the Council of the Evangelical Church appointed an Evangelical Film Officer and he did everything possible to assist in the making of the film, *Night Watch*, a successful and much discussed experiment in the category of religious films. Some time before, in October 1946, he had given a talk in German and English on this type of film from the platform of the local cinema in Büdingen, where he was then living, by way of introduction to the American feature film, *Going My Way*, in which Bing Crosby played the part of a sporting clergyman. It was a great event in the life of the small town. The Mayor had summoned the populace and the American occupation troops to the performance by sounding the air-raid warning and sending round a loudspeaker van. After the performance there was singing by the choir of the local boys' school and the cinema was crowded to the doors.

Though Niemöller himself claims to visit a cinema only once a year, there are plenty of witnesses amongst those nearest to him who assert that he is a more regular and enthusiastic "fan" than he would have us believe. When he was pastor of Dahlem he used to be a frequent filmgoer, accompanied usually by his wife and his assistant. Even today, memories of the veteran German comedians, Hans Moser and Theo Lingen, can make him laugh. His favourite film star in those days was the Austrian girl, Lucie Englisch, particularly in the film *The Country Girl*. More recently he has been seen to laugh at the Italian star, Sophia Loren, in *A Pity You're A Cad*—a film, incidentally, which has not aroused the unqualified enthusiasm of the clerical cinematic experts. Niemöller was particularly interested in the West German feature film, *The Captain from Köpenick*, in that it reminded him of his own imprisonment. The film apparently gave an accurate picture of prison life, for Niemöller left the cinema saying: "Yes, it was just like that."

While operas and plays seem "too long" for a man of Niemöller's impatient nature, he enjoys American musicals like *The Pajama Game* or *My Fair Lady*, and on his numerous American tours he takes care to leave room in his crowded programme for a visit to the latest New York musical, often finding time also to buy the music and some records of the hit tunes to take home with him for his family.

All these pastimes are in the nature of occasional relaxation. That applies also to reading for pleasure. Before Niemöller can get down to the latest German, American, or French novels, there are innumerable other duties, including obligatory reading to be done. Theological journals and the daily newspapers take up a good part of his spare time. Sometimes in the evenings when he is alone with his family he enjoys reading poetry aloud, usually from his favourite authors, Liliencron or Morgenstern, but never anything modern. Regularly he spends the last half-hour reading in bed. As in former years when composing his sermons, Niemöller likes to have a box of sweets within reach. The latest newspapers, among them the "chronique scandaleuse" of West Germany, *Der Spiegel*, are piled on his night-table. Sometimes the pile is topped by a book, open and face downwards. A while ago it was the Italian best-seller, *Don Camillo and Peppone*, which Niemöller found absorbing for its treatment of the inter-relations between the Church and politics.

Niemöller sees as much, or as little, of his family today as he did in the Münster years and during the Battle of the Churches. Now, as then, the days and most evenings are parcelled out in an unbroken succession of appointments and it is seldom indeed that he has leisure to be with his family after supper. As for having lunch at home—that virtually never happens. The

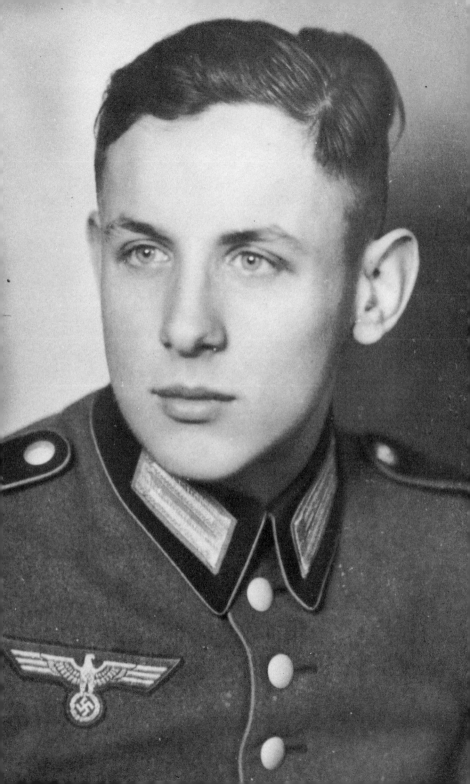

Niemöller's son Jochen, who was killed in the spring of 1945 family itself has shrunk. Niemöller's son Jochen was killed during the last few weeks of the war. His daughter, Jutta, died of diphtheria while he was still in the concentration camp. Brigitte, with three daughters of her own, lived in a south-west German town a three-hours train journey away before she took a job in the U.S.A. at the beginning of 1959. Hertha, who had previously been studying philosophy, married an official in the West German Foreign Office soon after returning from Moscow, where she had acted as her father's interpreter, and she and her husband now live in the Far East. Hermann is working as a doctor in the United States and his parents see him occasionally for half an hour when they are on one of their American tours. Johann Heinrich (Jan) has also left home. After returning from Russian captivity, he studied law for a while at Frankfurt University. He has now married a young schoolmistress and is working in local justice in Hessen. Martin, called Tini in the family, the youngest of the seven children, has also flown from the nest. After taking his school-leaving certificate at the classical secondary school in Wiesbaden like his brother Jan before him he decided to study law with the object of becoming a barrister, and he was among a number of young people who, assisted by Dr. Arndt, the legal adviser of the Social Democratic Party, charged the Bonn Government before the Federal Court in Karlsruhe with having infringed the West German Constitution by introducing military conscription. Tini's foster-brother, Hans Schulz, who is the same age as himself, is also passionately interested in politics. Hans has belonged to the family since the Büdingen days. He is training to be a trade buyer, but his ultimate aim is to become a journalist. He is a nephew of the indefatigable maid-of-all-work, Dora Schulz.

Anyone seeking information about the pastor and his family must not fail to consult Dora. A typical Berliner with her ready repartee and cheerful, resilient nature, Dora has been with the Niemöllers through all the ups and downs of the last twenty-five years. She knows all the friends and relations of the family and what others know only at second hand she can relate from personal experience. Originally Dora came for only a few weeks. She had intended to become a deaconess or teach at a kindergarten and it was only because no one else could be found that she had agreed to help out for a while at the vicarage.

Dora is a dainty, fair-haired little person who conceals amazing stamina and energy beneath her delicate exterior. When she first joined the family—the previous maid having left to get married after being with the Niemöllers for three years—she had no inkling of the formidable tasks that awaited her: seven children to help look after, fourteen rooms to clean, two telephones and a constantly ringing door-bell to answer and on top of all that, the cooking to do. "I didn't know whether I was on my head or my heels," she recalls today. "It was too much." After eight weeks she gave notice. "You can't do that!" the fifteen-year-old Jochen told her. "It's a dirty trick! Still, I suppose there are rather a lot of us. . . ." And Dora stayed. She is still with the Niemöllers today. In addition to all her other duties, she helped Frau Niemöller to bring up the children, a task which their father was glad to evade whenever any sternness was called for. "Mother, you do it. I don't want to have any arguments," he would say and withdraw to the security of his study. To the children he was "kind, but always in a hurry", says Dora, and she ought to know.

If there had been no Dora, Frau Niemöller would not have been able to accompany her husband on his foreign travels as she has done with increasing frequency during the past few years. Though she is fond of travel and states that it gives her great pleasure to accept the many invitations to lecture which she, too, receives, her main reason for going is that on their journeys abroad she can have her husband to herself for longer periods than is possible at home. Thus it came about that Frau Niemöller was with him during his first lecture tour in America in 1946 and also on several of the succeeding tours. She accompanied him to Australia, New Zealand, India, Britain,

France and many other countries. After all, she, too, has to make up for those eight years during which she was with him for a total of two days split into half-hour periods. During the time her husband was in the concentration camp Frau Niemöller must have suffered almost as much as he; if anything, perhaps more, for the spiritual issue was less clear-cut for her. Confronted daily with his S.S. guards and cut off from the outside world, the maintenance of morale was for Niemöller inseparable from survival. If he capitulated mentally, all hope would go and with hope gone, the life within him would become extinguished. But his wife was in a situation which did not automatically summon all her powers of resistance—on the contrary, her greatest danger was a kind of creeping despair which could not be ascribed to any one factor, but was due to a combination of prolonged uncertainty, the inability to help her husband directly, the slights and rebuffs to which she was continually exposed from ardent Nazis in all walks of life, and the knowledge that as long as the National Socialists were in control in Germany she and her family would remain under the blight of official displeasure. Moreover, Frau Niemöller took, and still takes, a strong personal interest in her husband's work and the sense of injustice rankled therefore no less strongly in her.

Because of her natural poise and dignity, Frau Niemöller is sometimes called "the queen" by friends of the family. In her early 'teens she taught for a while in England at a school in Tunbridge Wells. Niemöller has come increasingly during the course of the years to ask her opinion on all matters of importance.

The "*Herr Pastor*"—Niemöller, though Church President, still prefers this form of address when among friends—Frau Niemöller, Hans and Dora: these four comprise the family circle today, and they still observe the old custom of shaking hands at table after they have said grace together. Hardly a day passes without one of the Niemöller's other children being present or the grandchildren who live for months at a time with their grandparents. Frequently friends are present, or a journalist, perhaps, sent by his newspaper to collect material for a portrait of Niemöller. The latter is certain to be impressed by the lack of pretension in the household, and he is hardly likely to overlook the interests of readers avid for the "canine touch" by not mentioning Ratz, the dachshund, who has been with the family since an admiring lady presented him to Niemöller in 1946. Ratz enjoys a privileged position in the household. His welfare is the object of tender inquiries from his master when the latter is away, and his photograph is always in the master's wallet to remind him that there is at least one creature in the world who will never breathe a word of criticism. Ratz is allowed many liberties which more ordinary dogs would find entered against them in the Book of Fate. When Niemöller holds conferences with his fellow-clergy in his office with the bay window in Wiesbaden, Ratz claims and is conceded a large easy chair to himself. On such occasions he usually behaves with immense and impeccable solemnity, but in lighter moments Ratz has been known to act with scandalous disrespect, rending the diploma of an honorary doctorate conferred on his master and on the occasion of Niemöller's sixty-fifth birthday, seizing a large ham which a well-wisher had brought as a present and trailing it about among the guests in the reception room. Whether Ratz thought it was his birthday or whether in the absence of his master—who prefers to vanish on such occasions—the dog was trying to thank the donor of the ham on Niemöller's behalf, is a question which needs no answer, for those who know dogs will be able to think of other and more probable explanations. That outrage occurred in January, 1957, but since then Ratz has acquired a companion in the shape of another dachshund of somewhat more gentle birth, who has been given the name of Fratz and it is said that the presence of this elegant competitor for the favours of the family has done Ratz a power of good.

*   *   *

Dora, the housekeeper, and Ratz, the dachshund, both exert considerable influence in the Niemöller household

Niemöller, the "destroyer of his own reputation", is Protestant enough to know that he is no saint, not even the "un-
canonized saint" which American friends and admirers once declared him to be. Since 1945 many honours have been conferred
on him, honorary doctorates at Pine-Hill University in Halifax,
Canada (1946); Göttingen University, Germany (1946); New
Delhi University (1953); Bethany University of the Church of
Brethren, Chicago (1954); Budapest University (1955); London
University in West Ontario, Canada (1956) and the University
of Bratislava, Czechoslovakia (1956). In all these cases, with the
exception of New Delhi where he was made an honorary doctor
of philosophy, the doctorate conferred was that of Theology.
Finally New York University, with its 46,000 students, the
biggest privately controlled institution of higher education in
the world, conferred on Niemöller its bronze medal which had
been awarded only twice before since the university was founded
in 1831. Headed "Martin Niemöller—courageous churchman"
the citation read:

"Pastor Niemöller: You stand before us in the image of an un-
canonized saint of the church universal. One of the leading figures
in twentieth-century Christendom, in your valiant defence of the
Faith against unspeakable atheistic desecration and tyranny,
utterly fearless and disdainful of retributive torture and confinement, you fired the imagination, quickened the hopes and lifted
the hearts of reverential fellow men the world over. We now stand
before you, therefore, in humble respect and gratitude. You
honour us, Sir, with your presence, and we bid you Godspeed
upon your dedicated mission by conferring upon you the official
medal of New York University."

In returning thanks for this, as for most other honours conferred
on him, Niemöller stressed that he accepted it, not for himself
but in the name of all those who had achieved and suffered more
for the Church than he had. To his friends Niemöller has said
that his fame is too great in view of those martyrs who suffered
long torture and died cruel deaths and are now almost forgotten.

Be this as it may, there is plenty of evidence to suggest that Niemöller has as yet no intention of retiring, unlike many churchmen of his age. "If you want to get rid of me, then I shall go to East Germany and work in a small village somewhere," he declared before a recent Synod at which his right to speak out as a Christian was challenged. That was no rhetorical gesture, he meant it seriously, as he did in the winter of 1952 in Moscow when he asked in vain for permission to stay in Russia as chaplain with the German prisoners-of-war. He has also discussed more than once with his intimate friends the possibility of going on a long evangelizing tour in the United States and other parts of the world when his term as Church President ends*. Strange as it may seem, such plans are not prompted by impatience or the restlessness which Niemöller's character has always revealed. Apart from the fact that this is not so apparent to his friends as formerly, his faith as a Christian prevents him from trying to take life by storm. Not that his friends and supporters would resent Niemöller striking out on some new path; on the contrary, they are convinced that there are many new tasks awaiting him and that he has still plenty to say. Why, some of them ask, does he not go in for politics? There is a desperate need of men like him in public life. The field is open and he has all the qualities required.

Niemöller pays no heed to these voices. He has always refused to abandon his life in the Church and he believes he is destined to remain in it. Though his protest, "I am not a politician" aroused incredulous laughter, he meant it and he still means it, for whenever he has entered the political arena, either under Hitler or since the Second World War, it has been the proclaiming of Christ's Message and not political ambition which has urged him to do so. Now, as the wheel comes full circle and fresh aspects of life are revealed to a mind tempered by age and experience, none of this has changed, but rather Niemöller

* In March 1958 Niemöller was re-elected by a majority of two votes for a further term of eight years.

Dr. Rajendra Prasad, President of India, bestowing an honorary doctor's degree of the University of New Delhi on Pastor Niemöller (1953) appears to be aware of the path he must tread more clearly than ever before. He is still very much a man of the moment, but in a very different sense than applies to most of those in Church or politics whom the newspapers lump together under the term, "dignitaries". If Niemöller were cynical and ambitious enough to subscribe to the taboos now current in both spheres of life, and in the relations between them, he could acquire a secure and accepted place in the ranks of the "dignitaries". But it seems to the unbiased observer that Niemöller is coming to sense with increasing certainty that the role of a servant of Christ cannot be reconciled with that of "dignitary". If he became a politician he would betray himself, as he would no less if he condescended to strike the bargain that is usually made in Western Europe—and not only there—between Church and State and which consists in each recognizing and seeking to establish the other's position.

The path which Niemöller seems to be treading with even greater resolve than before is narrower, harder, more controversial and more open to misunderstanding. It is too early to judge, but it appears unlikely that Niemöller's path will be the same as Tolstoy's, as a voice from America suggests. At any rate, if all the signs are to be believed, it will hardly be the path of outward power and cheap popularity. It will make heavy demands on him who treads it, but it will not lead him to the loneliness of isolation so long as he remains a member of that Christian fellowship from which, rather than from a clerical despotism, Niemöller foresaw long ago, in 1934, that the salvation of the Evangelical Church would one day be forthcoming.

BIOGRAPHICAL NOTES

ADENAUER, KONRAD, DR. Born 1876. 1917-1933 and 1945-1949, Mayor of Cologne. Since 1949 Chancellor of the West German Federal Republic. Re-elected 1953 and 1957. The only personal meeting between Niemöller and Adenauer took place in 1950 at a discussion between the Chancellor and the leaders of the Evangelical Church concerning the effect of West German rearmament on the re-unification of Germany.

ASMUSSEN, HANS. A close colleague of Niemöller's during the Battle of the Churches, when he was Pastor of a Berlin parish. Later Dean of Kiel. 1945-1950, Head of Chancery of German Evangelical Church. Now living in Heidelberg.

BARTH, KARL, D.D., LL.D., Professor, Dr. of Theology. Born 1886. Swiss theologian, with his *Commentary on the Epistle to the Romans* (1918) a co-founder of the so-called "Dialectical Theology". Was Professor of Systematic Theology in Bonn during the first phase of the Battle of the Churches. In 1934 was discharged from German State service for refusing to swear an oath of allegiance to Hitler. 1935, went to Basle. At present working on his comprehensive *Ecclesiastical Dogmatics*.

BODELSCHWINGH, FRIEDRICH VON. 1831-1910. Administered the Institutes of the Home Mission in Bethel, near Bielefeld, Westphalia, which were later named after him and in which sick persons of all kinds were given a permanent home, especially epileptics. As a member of the Prussian State Assembly took up the cause of casual labourers and of the unemployed. Under the motto *Arbeit statt Almosen* (Work not Alms) founded the first workers' colonies in Germany.

EHLERS, HERMANN, DR. Born 1904, died 1954. Lawyer. Member of the Oldenburg Board of Consistory. During the Hitler period, legal adviser to the Confessing Church. After 1945, member of the West German Federal Assembly (Christian Democratic Union). 1950, elected President of the Federal Assembly.

214

FRICK, WILHELM. Born 1877. One of the first supporters of Adolf Hitler. 1924, Member of the Reichstag. 1929-1931, Minister of the Interior for Thuringia (first National Socialist Minister in a German Provincial Government). 1933, Reich Minister of the Interior. 1943, Reich Protector of Bohemia and Moravia. 1946, sentenced to death by hanging by the International Military Tribunal in Nürnberg and executed.

GOEBBELS, JOSEPH, DR. Born 1897. Studied literary history and history. Editor of National Socialist newspapers. 1926, "Gauleiter", i.e. Party Leader for Berlin of National Socialist German Workers' Party. 1929, Head of Reich's Propaganda Department for the N.S. Party. When Hitler became Chancellor, appointed Minister for Propaganda and Public Enlightenment. Author of numerous books, including *Vom Kaiserhof zur Reichskanzlei*. Committed suicide with his family in Hitler's Bunker in Berlin on 1 May, 1945.

GOERING, HERMANN. Born 1893. In the First World War commander of the Richthofen Squadron. Awarded Iron Cross and the *"Pour le Mérite"*, the highest German award for bravery. Early supporter of Hitler, standing next to him in the latter's abortive Munich Putsch in 1923, when Goering was severely wounded. 1932, elected President of the Reichstag. 1933, Prime Minister of Prussia, Minister of Air, Chief Forester of the Reich. Later, Marshal of the Reich. Shortly before the Capitulation in 1945, fell under Hitler's suspicion as wishing to succeed him and stripped of all his offices of state. 1946, sentenced to death by the Nürnberg International Military Tribunal, but committed suicide.

HAHN, OTTO, Professor. Born 1879. Awarded Nobel Prize for Chemistry in 1944. Since 1946, President of the Max Planck Society. Together with Fritz Stassmann discovered the nuclear chain reaction on first splitting the Uranium atom. One of 18 West German atomic scientists who in April, 1957, gave public warning of the disastrous consequences of an atomic war, and refused on grounds of conscience to assist in the development and manufacture of atomic weapons for the German Federal Republic.

HEUSS, THEODOR, Prof. Dr. Born 1884. 1924-1933 Democratic member of German Reichstag. 1945-6, Minister of Culture in Württemberg-Baden. 1948-49, Chairman of the Free Democratic Party. 1949, elected by the West German Federal Assembly (Bundestag) to be first President of the West German Federal Republic. Re-elected 17th July, 1954, in Berlin.

HOOFT, VISSER'T, W. A., DR. Born in Haarlem, Holland, 1900. Member of the Dutch Reformed Church. President of the World Student Christian Federation. 1938, General Secretary of the Provisional Committee of the Ecumenical Council. 1948, General Secretary of the World Council of Churches.

KLEPPER, JOCHEN. Born 1903. Son of a Silesian pastor. His biography of King Frederick William I of Prussia, *Der Vater* (The Father), placed him in the front rank of Protestant writers. Committed suicide in 1942 with his wife and her daughter by her first marriage when the last-named was about to be put in a concentration camp on account of Jewish parentage. Klepper's diaries of the years 1932 to 1942 have been published by the Deutsche Verlags-Anstalt under the title *Unter dem Schatten deiner Flügel* (Under the Shadow of Thy Wings).

MCCARTHY, JOSEPH. Born 1909, died 1957. Republican Senator in U.S.A. Received a vote of censure from the Senate for the methods he employed as Chairman of the Senatorial Committee for the Investigation of Communist Activities.

NOSKE, GUSTAV. Social-Democratic politician. 1868-1946. 1906, member of the German Reichstag. 1919, instrumental in the suppression of the Spartacist uprising in Berlin. First Defence Minister of the Weimar Republic. 1920-1933, President of Hanover.

ROSENBERG, ALFRED. Born 1893. 1921, Editor of the National Socialist newspaper, *Völkischer Beobachter*. 1923, participated in Hitler's abortive Munich Putsch. 1930, member of the Reichstag. 1933, Head of Foreign Affairs Department of the Nazi Party and "Reichsleiter". A profuse writer obsessed by hatred of the Jews and hate of racial admixture. Became the Nazi Party's ideologist with his book, *The Myth of the Twentieth Century*, published in 1930 and which sold a million copies. 1941, Reich Minister for the Occupied Territories in the East. 1946, condemned by the International Military Tribunal in Nürnberg and executed.

SCHACHT, HJALMAR, DR. Born 1877. 1923, Reich Food Commissar, President of the Reichsbank. 1934-39, Reich Minister of Economics, fell into disfavour and was sent in 1944 to Dachau concentration camp. In 1946 was acquitted by the International Military Tribunal in Nürnberg of complicity in war crimes. In a letter to Martin Niemöller dated 31st January, 1957, thanking the latter for his good wishes on the occasion of his eightieth birthday, Dr. Schacht wrote: "Amongst more than one thousand messages of congratulation which have reached me on my eightieth birthday, your own is one of those which have given me particular pleasure. When I think of my time in Dahlem, your personality always stands vividly before me, and when I remember those weeks between Dachau and Naples it is once again our common lot which prevails. Since then our paths have separated, though remaining inwardly the same. It must be a source of great satisfaction to you to have persevered in your course despite the enmities that have arisen.

Neither you nor I have lacked critics or efforts to silence us. But our North German natures have helped us calmly to surmount our difficulties. Even among those who share the same views one may disagree on points of detail in political discussion, but the broad line of policy remains clear—the preservation of the German virtues, the pursuit of justice and decency, the attainment of peace with honour, and the maintenance of the link with the Eternal."

SCHUMACHER, KURT, DR. 1895-1952. 1930, member of the German Reichstag. 1933-1954 in a concentration camp. 1945, Chairman of the Social Democratic Party. 1949, member of the West German Federal Assembly.

TURNER, EWART E. 1930-1934, Pastor of the American Church in Berlin. Since 1934 correspondent of the *Religious News Service*. Friend of the Confessing Church and a close friend of Niemöller's. 1939, forced to leave Germany. Returned in 1945 with the U.S. Forces as Religious Affairs Officer in Military Government. A farewell message which he sent to his friends in the Confessing Church before finally leaving Germany for the United States in December, 1945, contained the sentence: "You are writing Church history for centuries to come."

BIBLIOGRAPHY

BARTH, KARL. *Zum Kirchenkampf* (*Theol. Existenz heute*, No. 49). Chr. Kaiser Verlag, Munich, 1956.

BEKENNENDE KIRCHE. *Martin Niemöller zum* 60 *Geburtstag.* Chr. Kaiser Verlag, Munich, 1952.

BEYER, FRANZ. *Menschen warten. Aus dem politischen Wirken Martin Niemöllers seit* 1945. Wilhelm Schneider Verlag, Siegen, 1952.

BOEHM, ERICH. *We Survived.* The stories of 14 of the Hidden and the Hunted. Yale University Press, 1949.

FRANKE, WALTER. *Deutsches Christentum und deutsche Reichskirche als Forderung der Gegenwart.* Verlag Moritz Diesterweg, Frankfurt a.M., 1933.

KLINGLER, FRITZ (ED.). *Dokumente zum Abwehrkampf der deutschen evangelischen Pfarrerschaft.*

KONSTANTIN, *Prinz von Bayern. Die grossen Namen.* Kindler Verlag, 1956.

KURZ, A. *Bekennende Kirche.* Verlag Haus und Schule, Berlin, 1946.

NIEMÖLLER, MARTIN. *Vom U-Boot zur Kanzel*, Martin Warneck Verlag, Berlin, 1934.

(British Edition, *From U-boat to Pulpit*, Constable, 1934.)

... *zu verkündigen, ein gnädiges Jahr des Herrn! Sechs Dachauer Predigten.* Ev. Verlag AG, Zollikon, 1946 (also published in English: Six Dachau Sermons.)

Wir predigen den gekreuzigten Christus. Ev. Verlag, Zollikon-Zürich, 1949.

Herr, wohin sollen wir gehen? Predigten. Chr. Kaiser Verlag, Munich, 1956.

Reden 1955-1957. Verlag "Stimme der Gemeinde", Darmstadt, 1957.

NIEMÖLLER, WILHELM. *Martin Niemöller. Ein Lebensbild.* Chr. Kaiser Verlag, 1952.

Macht geht vor Recht. Der Prozess Martin Niemöllers. Chr. Kaiser Verlag, 1952.

Die Evangelische Kirche im Dritten Reich, Handbuch des Kirchenkampfes, Ludwig Bechauf Verlag, Bielefeld, 1956.

SCHREY, HEINZ HORST. *Die Generation der Entscheidung, Staat und Kirche in Europa und im Europäischen Russland,* 1918-1953. Chr. Kaiser Verlag, Munich, 1955.

STUCKELBERGER, HANS MARTIN. *Der Kampf der Bekennenden Kirche und Martin Niemöller, von der Schweiz aus gesehen, Verlag der Evangelischen Gesellschaft,* St. Gallen, Switzerland, 1945.

WIEN, DEKAN. *Zur Stuttgarter Erklärung, Evangelische Buchhandlung Rud.* Senftleben, Kaiserslautern (undated).

WOLF, ERNST. *Barmen. Kirche zwischen Versuchung und Gnade.* Chr. Kaiser. Verlag München, 1957.

(ANONYMOUS.) *Ein National-Sozialistischer Funktionär zum Niemöller-Prozess* (In: *Vierteljahrshefte für Zeitgeschichte,* No. 3/1956, Deutsche Verlags-Anstalt, Stuttgart.)

Martin Niemöller und sein Bekenntnis, pub. Schweizer Evangelisches Hilfswerk für die Bekennende Kirche in Deutschland, Verlag der Evangelischen Buchhandlung, Zollikon, 1939.

Also letters, sermons, lectures, pamphlets, articles and reports in German and foreign newspapers and periodicals.

INDEX

Academic Defence Corps, 66, 67
Adenauer, Doctor, 168, 174, 175, 182, 186, 195, 214
Alexander, Field-Marshal, 136
Armistice (First World War), 58, 59
Asmussen, Hans, 138, 214

Barth, Karl, 97, 142, 144, 180, 181, 214, 218
Bartning, Ludwig, 100, 121
Berggrav, Bishop, 152
Best, Major, 125, 133
Bodelschwingh, Frederick von, 74, 98, 154, 214
Bodelschwingh Institutions, 87
Bonin, von, Colonel, 130–2
Bonn Assembly, 165, 191
Bremer, Else, 35, 49, 56, 61
Bremer, Hermann, 35, 49
Britannic, 43

Catholic Church, 122, 123, 161, 177
Catholicism, 123–5, 127
Chichester, Bishop of, 90, 104
Christian Democratic Union, 168, 175, 187
Christian Occident, 171
Church of Saint Paul, 160
Communism, 65–7, 151, 171, 172, 181, 182, 201
Confessing Church, 97–100, 103, 107–10, 112, 122, 141–4, 152, 162, 187
Consistory Board, 75, 76, 80
Council of the Brethren of the Confessing Church, 163, 164, 173, 176

Council of the Brethren of the German Evangelical Church, 98
Council of the Evangelical Church, 147, 173, 176, 183, 188

Dachau, 123–38, 144, 150
Dahlem, 81, 83, 88, 98, 99, 104, 115, 122, 136, 137, 143, 145, 156, 158, 165, 196
Declaration of Barmen, 161
De-Nazification, 159, 160, 168, 175
Dibelius, Doctor, 124, 147, 154, 183

Ecumenical Council, 90, 148, 152, 157
Eisenach Conference, July 1948, 162, 163
Eisenach Declaration, 172
Eisenhower, General, later President, 138, 170
Elberfeld, 24, 35, 55, 61, 72, 82, 120
European Defence Organization, 180
Evangelical Savings Society, 75
Evangelical Union, 1817, 77

Federal Committee of Young German Democrats, 182
Federal Council of the Churches of Christ, 154
Francis Joseph, Emperor, 42
Frick, Wilhelm, 92, 215,

Ghandhi-ism, 185, 186
General Synod for Prussia, 89

German Christians Movement, 85–9, 91, 96, 98–100, 104, 105, 107, 122, 123, 141
German Evangelical Church, 86–9, 142, 144, 145, 148, 157, 161, 178, 187, 192
German Federal Republic, 172
German Nationals, 66
German Pastors' Union, 120, 122
German Protestant Churches, 86, 90, 96, 97
Gestapo, 91, 92, 94, 100–4, 112, 113, 117, 119, 120, 122, 125
Gloucester, Bishop of, 105
Goebbels, Joseph, Doctor, 109, 146, 215
Goering, Hermann, 92–4, 151, 215
Great Church of Saint Mary, 14

Hahn, Otto, Professor, 170, 215
Hamburg Synod, April 1951, 179
Haug, Doctor, 168
Heinemann, Gustav, Doctor, 168, 169, 174, 180, 182, 183, 187, 188
Hertha, 28–31, 34–6, 42
Hessen-Nassau Church, 111, 161, 185, 197, 198
Heuss, Theodor, Doctor, Professor, 179, 180, 215
Hildebrandt, Franz, Doctor, 122
Himmler, 133
Hindenburg, President, 88, 92
Hitler, Adolf, 70, 85–9, 91–7, 99, 109–11, 116–8, 120–7, 129, 130, 132–4, 136, 140–3, 155, 159, 162, 164, 172, 178, 196, 212
House of Hohenzollern, 18

Inflation, 68–70

July Plot, 130
Jung, C.G., 121
Jutland, Battle of, 42

Kähler, Pastor, 71
Kaiser, 18, 19, 30, 31, 58
Kapp, 66
Kapp *Putsch*, 66, 67
Kiel, 27–9, 35, 37, 38, 42, 57–9, 61, 85
Klepper, Jochen, 98, 216
Koch, Doctor, 89, 95
Korea, 166, 170

League of Nations, 96
Leoni, 138, 140, 142, 144, 147, 153
Lippstadt, 14, 20, 22–5, 75
Lufft, Hans, 68
Lumb, Doctor, 25
Luther, Martin, 18, 23, 68, 85, 89, 104, 156, 177
Lutheran Churches, 77, 96, 98, 101, 143, 153, 156, 161, 162, 189
Lutheran Synod of Hanover, 177

Martin Niemöller and his Creed, 122
Marxism, 163
Meiser, Doctor, 153, 187, 188
Müller, Ludwig, 86–8, 90–2, 94
Münster, 20, 64–7, 70, 71, 75, 76, 81, 125, 145, 204
Mussolini, 133

National Socialism, 85, 86, 96, 112, 115, 122, 155
National Socialist Party, 70, 85, 149, 151, 209
Nazi Party, 10, 85, 87, 96, 104–6, 121, 124, 126, 127, 135, 144, 153
New Teaching, 23
Niemöller, Christine, 16
Niemöller, Gerhard, 15, 16
Niemöller, Heinrich, 16–25, 119, 120

Niemöller, Martin, children of, 67, 68, 78

Niemöller, Martin, honours conferred upon, 211

Niemöller, Paula (nee Müller), 20, 21, 22

Noske, Gustav, 58, 216

Nürnberg Tribunal, 137

Open Air Campaigners, 156

Pan-European Movement, 170

Pastors' Emergency Union, 89–91, 93–5, 98

Potsdam Agreement, 167

Protestant Churches, Battle of, 84, 85, 95, 96, 112, 124, 142, 159, 161, 202, 206

Protestant Home Mission, 73–5, 78, 80, 81, 87, 158

Provincial Synod, 75

Raeder, Grand Admiral, 120–2

Rationing, 64

Redeemer, Church of the, Münster, 75

Reichs Council of Brethren, 142

Reichswehr, 67, 68

Republican State, 62

Roosevelt, Eleanor, Mrs., 121, 155, 203

Rosenburg, Alfred, 96, 97, 112, 216

Saint Anne, Church of, Dahlem, 83, 104

Sachsenhausen, 115–8, 120, 124

Sauerbruch, Professor, 110, 113

Schacht, Hjalmar, Doctor, 125, 130, 216

Schliepstein, Pastor, 14, 15

Schweitzer, Albert, 76

Siess, Kapitänleutnant, 38, 39, 41, 43, 44, 45

Social Democrat Party, 160, 175, 182, 192, 207

Stevens, Major, 125, 136

Stratenwerth, Gerhard, 87, 154

Stuttgart Declaration, 148–52, 160, 168, 203

Synod, Berlin-Weissensee, April 1950, 173

Synod of Bethel, January, 1949, 162, 163, 173

Synod of Espelkamp, 1955, 188

Synod of the Evangelical Church of Hessen and Nassau, 157, 158, 176, 177, 184, 187

Synod of the German Evangelical Church, 1957, 191

Thomas, General, 130, 132

Thüringen, 36, 37

Treysa Conference, 1945, 161

U-Boats, 38–48, 50–9

Unemployment, 85

Union for Democratic Control, 180

United Evangelical Lutheran Churches of Germany, 161, 162, 178, 189

United German People's Party, 187

Waldensians, 31

Waldus, Petrus, 31

Wehrmacht, 132

Weimar Constitution, 65, 66

Weimar Republic, 64

Wersen, 15, 16, 20, 62

Westerkappeln, 20, 61–3, 65

Westermann, Johann, 23

West German Federal Assembly, 174, 176, 196

West German Federal Republic, 167, 169, 171, 172, 187, 192

West German State, 167

Westphalia, 14, 15, 20, 21, 23, 33, 61, 74, 76, 78, 81, 97, 122
Wichern, Johann Hinrich, 73
Wilhelmshaven, 36, 37
Wittenburg, 18, 23, 68
Wittenburg National Synod, 89

World Conference of Christian Youth, 157, 185
World Conference of Churches, Evanston, 1954, 170

Zeppelin, L. 23, 49